WOMEN, WHISTLEBLOWING, WIKILEAKS

WOMEN, WHISTLEBLOWING, WIKILEAKS

RENATA AVILA,
SARAH HARRISON AND
ANGELA RICHTER

OR Books
New York · London

Published by OR Books, New York and London
Visit our website at www.orbooks.com

First printing 2017

Cataloging-in-Publication data is available from the Library of Congress. A catalog record for this book is available from the British Library.

ISBN 978-1-682191-16-3 paperback
ISBN 978-1-682191-17-0 e-book

This book is set in the typeface Minion Pro
Typeset by AarkMany Media Pvt. Ltd., Chennai, India.
Printed by BookMobile in the United States and CPI Books Ltd in the United Kingdom.

CONTENTS

To Michael Ratner and Gavin MacFadyen

We pledge to continue the trouble you wanted to
see in the world.

FOREWORD: THE DUSK OF MALE BACKROOM POLITICS

The idea for this book originated in 2013 at the celebration of the European Center for Constitutional and Human Rights (ECCHR) in Berlin. It was there that I met Sarah Harrison who, three days previously, had returned from Moscow where she had spent several months with the NSA whistleblower Edward Snowden. I had known Sarah for two years as a result of my work with WikiLeaks and its founder Julian Assange. Sarah was the closest of collaborators, trusted by Assange and a passionate journalist with WikiLeaks. She had travelled to Hong Kong for the organization and had helped Edward Snowden escape after his announcement that he was the NSA whistleblower. She intervened as his situation was becoming increasingly difficult. By the time she arrived in Hong Kong, Snowden was on his own. The filmmaker Laura Poitras and the journalist Glenn Greenwald had already left the city, as had the journalists from the *Guardian* and the *Washington Post*, who departed with the NSA documents in their baggage.

Snowden's stay in Hong Kong, documented by Poitras in the Oscar-winning film "Citizenfour", was actually only the beginning of a real life espionage thriller that took place between Hong Kong and Moscow. Sarah's intervention was a classic David versus Goliath story: One woman against the global reach of the USA, the world's greatest superpower. With the help of Assange, who was by then already confined to asylum in the Ecuadorian embassy, Sarah managed to outsmart the mightiest secret service in the world to rescue Snowden. She stayed with him after the successful escape to Moscow, first for weeks in a windowless room in the transit zone of Moscow's Sheremetyevo airport, and then for many more months in the city. She did not leave for her voluntary exile in Berlin until she knew that Snowden was safe.

Sarah and I were planning to get together for a talk about whistleblowing, WikiLeaks, and Snowden. I asked her about the possibility of publishing our conversation on 60pages.com. Sarah said she liked the idea, but wanted to think about it for a few days. In the end we decided to invite another friend to join our discussion, Guatemalan human rights lawyer Renata Avila, who had been helping Julian Assange legally for years and who is also one of the trustees of the Snowden defense fund, where she works on strategies and campaigns aimed at keeping him safe and secure.

The idea was to bring together a trio of women from different backgrounds and parts of the world for a conversation about an area of activity that is widely perceived as heavily male dominated: whistleblowing and digital dissidence. This is an impression that is fostered by the mainstream media that focuses heavily on key male players in the field, most notably, of course, Snowden and Assange, as well as the journalist Glenn Greenwald. Chelsea Manning is a notable exception in this, although in spite of the fact that she has spoken publicly about her life as a transgender woman, she is still referred to widely as "he" in a largely unsympathetic press.

It's been striking to me that, in my years of working in the world of digital activism, from WikiLeaks to a diverse range of internet groups, women are active and hold important positions, yet are seldom prominent. This is not because women lack the assertiveness to occupy a role in the foreground, as is so often claimed with a certain paternalism. It stems, in part, from the unwillingness of mainstream media to appreciate and fairly report the role of women in digital activism. How else can one explain the description in the German weekly *Der Spiegel* (to just take one prominent example) of Sarah Harrison after her return to Europe from Moscow as an "assistant" or "friend" of Assange, instead of describing her as a brave, independent journalist?

The good news is that we are approaching the dusk of male backroom politics. It is the downfall of a whole epoch marked by widely accepted public lies, of clandestine dealings and the corruption that is so common in the circles of the powerful in business, politics, and the secret services. WikiLeaks is only the forerunner in this battle against male backroom politics, one that promises to fundamentally change our world as we enter the era of transparency that stretches out in front of us. It is by now, thanks to technology, nearly impossible to keep any kind of scheming hidden forever. Consider the various leaks and scandals that have hit the NSA, FIFA, BND, the Vatican and Volkswagen – the times of fiction are forever over. At this moment, the revelations of digital activism are still being treated as akin to the scandals of the 20th century, crises crises, which come and go, fired up by the media without ever fulfilling their revolutionary potential.

This is because there still is no name for this new onslaught of events. It represents only the beginning and a warning to the leaders in business, politics and the secret services that it now takes only one person to stand up to their power. If just one person reveals a few truths that are obvious to everybody who wants to see and hear them, the scheming is over. Secrecy has been the condition for keeping their power intact, a power that is now under significant threat.

In light of recent events, including Donald Trump's election, the proliferation of so called "fake news," as well as the latest terrorist attacks in Germany and Turkey, the topics discussed here seem ever more urgent.

Angela Richter, May 2017

WOMEN, WHISTLEBLOWING, WIKILEAKS: A DISCUSSION

FROM PASSIVE RECIPIENTS TO ACTIVE PARTICIPANTS

Joseph Farrell (JF) facilitated the discussion. He is a WikiLeaks journalist and its ambassador.

JF   What I want to do first is to talk to each of you about what motivated you to become politically active. I want to understand how each of you went from being – which I imagine you all were at some point – passive recipients of dogma to active political participants. That is, how did you end up being one of these women around this table? OK, Angela?

AR   For me, it was very simple. I was very politically aware when I was growing up. I was particularly influenced in this regard by my father, who was a political dissident in Yugoslavia. And then later, I became an artist. I studied theater directing and became part of an art collective that was very influenced by the Situationist International.[1] For several years I was quite satisfied with solely making art, but at some point I realized that I wasn't interested

1.   The Situationist International was an organization of social revolutionaries founded in 1957 comprising avant-garde artists, intellectuals and political theorists. See: https://archive.is/lL45N

in self-absorption and self-expression like many of my colleagues. I was more interested in engaging politically with society, rather than focusing on my own subjectivity, which was and maybe still is the most popular subject for contemporary artists. I even became quite depressed when I realized that my artwork was simply entertaining the bourgeoisie, wealthy art lovers. I really got depressed doing Shakespeare.

Then WikiLeaks happened. I was astonished when I first became aware of WikiLeaks. It was based on such a simple, yet compelling and powerful idea: an anonymous portal, a 'baby hatch,' for releasing classified government and corporate documents that would help ordinary people to hold the powerful to account. At the same time, I had become aware that the classical forms of activism just didn't work anymore. It seemed to me that the Western governments will quite happily let the protesters demonstrate, knowing that such demonstrations will not be able to effect meaningful change. I came to see that people can protest for weeks or months, maybe even years, but that it will never seem to really change anything. At least, that was how I felt about it. Even the Occupy movement,[2] which I found very impressive when it started, eventually petered out without causing significant change at the levels of corporate and governmental institutions. But at some point I thought, "It'll just peter out." So when WikiLeaks happened, I was really fascinated, as it seemed to be so much more

2.   A worldwide leaderless social protest movement, which grew out of the Spanish Indignados movement and the impact of the Arab Spring. See: https://archive.is/Ubdzl; and Occupy Wall Street website: https://archive.is/LZuOp

effective than typical protest tactics. I thought to myself: "This is now something that really works." I was so fascinated and excited about WikiLeaks. That's why I decided to make a play about it. On the other hand, web-based activism clearly has a serious downside. People have switched from congregating in public spaces, to express their opinions and engage in political discussion, to having these conversations on online platforms. What makes this shift so alarming is that the platforms are owned and controlled by private entities, so now a great deal of political debate takes place not at rallies or on the street but on Twitter, on Facebook, on Google - all of them private platforms. But nonetheless I got sucked into it. So that's how it happened. I, myself, increasingly came to engage increasingly in web-based activism.

JF   How did you become politically active Renata?

RA   For me, a crucial day was January 1st 1994, my thirteenth birthday. At exactly the moment when I was entering my teens, the Zapatista Revolution erupted right next door in the state of Chiapas, in the Southern part of Mexico, very close to my own country - Guatemala. Back then, Guatemala was still a country at war. Angela discussed earlier about how traditional forms of activism were no longer working in the West. But where I come from those forms of political action never worked effectively. All political opposition since the Rebel efforts in the Guatemalan Civil War was simply crushed and huge swathes of those more marginalized sectors of the population were always left out of the picture politically. At that time the Guatemalan Genocide[3] had already left more than

3. See Guatemalan Civil War: https://archive.is/HlP5w

7

200,000 killed, 50,000 disappeared and more than 1,500,000 refugees.

And then suddenly, unexpectedly, thousands of masked, armed, indigenous peasants - the Zapatistas - took control of a huge territory, and forced the world to pay attention to their cause and their demands. I can only mentally revisit the experience of seeing the Zapatista uprising emerge now. But I wish I had kept a diary about my impressions back then. You see the world with very different eyes when you are only 13 years old, but I guess I have not changed much since then. I still have the same sparkle in my eyes when I see real revolutionary change happening.

What was distinctive and new about the Zapatistas was that they managed to defeat the information blockade that surrounded them by using the internet. The government had thrown a military cordon around the liberated zone and, consequently, the press had no access to the area. Yet Zapatistas, by communicating with the outside world using the internet, managed to undermine and defeat the official government narrative of what was going on in Chiapas. The Zapatistas were among the first political actors to show the world new forms of communication to aid autonomous organizing. And this digitally-assisted underground revolution that was taking place just across the border from my country, and the international support it drew, really fascinated me. And so I paid close attention to the leading voices of the Zapatistas, following the figure of Subcomandante Marcos,[4] and the courageous and brilliant Comandante Ramona.[5]

4. See 'Profile: The Zapatistas' mysterious leader', *BBC News*: https://archive.is/dk2k

5. See footnote 3.

I was also struck by the impressive level of international solidarity the Zapatistas inspired, that helped to foster and protect the unique uprising in Chiapas.[6] After following the situation closely from Guatemala, I was able to gain a better understanding of the uprising when I visited Chiapas with a family friend who was working there for the Red Cross. As a consequence of that visit, I felt its authenticity. I decided to go to law school in order to engage in human rights law, instead of doing biochemistry, even though my skills were stronger in science. My heart was, and is, in the humanities.

The second thing that propelled me into political activism was my experience of a different encounter with 'truth'. I was working as a lawyer representing indigenous victims of genocide and other human rights abuses; included in the victims was the prominent indigenous leader, Nobel Peace Prize Laureate Rigoberta Menchu Tum.[7] In order to prepare the evidence of the case, I had to collect testimonies, coordinate technical and scientific expert reports, and cross-examine individuals involved with the materials and cases published by the Truth Commission in Guatemala.[8] When I was doing my work, it was only 10 years after the signing of the misnamed '*Guatemalan*

6. See 'Twenty Years Since the Chiapas Rebellion: The Zapatistas, Their Politics, and Their Impact', Solidarity-US.org: https://archive.is/qGb5f
7. Nobel Peace Prize 1992, Rigoberta Menchú Tum – Facts: https://archive.is/lAjBy
8. From 1997 to 1999 in Guatemala the Commission for Historical Clarification was created to clarify human rights violations related to the 36-year internal conflict from 1960 to the United Nations' brokered peace agreement of 1996, and to foster tolerance and preserve memory of the victims. The Commission presented its final report *Guatemala: Memory of Silence* (*Guatemala: Memoria del Silencio*) on 25 February 1999. See: https://archive.is/b9SMY

Accord for a firm and lasting peace'. I am not joking about the name. It was my first encounter with contrasting accounts of the Guatemalan civil war – the story of a terrible war as narrated by the oppressed victims and the perpetrators. It was my first experience of working closely with the victims as well as with indigenous lawyers. Also, it was the first time I had to deal with the extreme corruption of the Guatemalan judiciary and the ways in which the law is manipulated in the interests of the powerful.

I was shocked to see how my government had constantly lied to me, and to all Guatemalans. I was also shocked by how broken and fraudulent our education system and media were. And I was also disturbed by how ineffective the response of the international community was to the crimes of the Guatemalan elite. During my childhood and my teenage years I never heard about the atrocities of the civil war. I never knew about the 1,500,000 displaced Guatemalan refugees living in misery in the South of Mexico. I didn't know, about the killing of children (some of them smashed against trees to save on bullets, others killed while they were still inside their mothers' wombs), about the disappearances, torture, and public killing of most of the indigenous leaders. And I hadn't understood how I had been living a lie: how I was going to law school with the sons and daughters of war criminals, and of really corrupt politicians and businessmen. I was simply pretending that everything was ok, whilst I enjoyed the fruits of a rotten system. There are few elites as racist, ignorant, corrupt and brutal as the Guatemalan ones, for whom rules do not apply.

There is no such thing as international law or human rights in Guatemala with respect to those who control the country. There are no fundamental rights. There are just powerful, entrenched interests that will block any efforts by and for the people. I worked with excellent litigators, as good as any lawyers in the world, solid as rock, who met all national and international legal standards. But when the powerful are the accused, it is not enough. With the complicity of the media, the voice of the powerful becomes the voice of 'truth'. And it's one thing to have the documents that expose the abusers; the real struggle is getting the press to actually publish them and effect some real change.

When I first met Julian Assange, one of the first things we discussed was how, in some situations, it's not a question of evidence being leaked – it doesn't need to be leaked, it is already out there in the public domain. The balance of powers in our societies is such that elites are not affected by the availability of such evidence. I was really frustrated by the justice system in Guatemala but somehow I still had high hopes for the international legal system. The event that really changed my opinion regarding international law was the Gaza massacres at the end of 2008, called Operation Cast Lead. I could not believe that even though we were witnessing a massacre in real-time, committed by a supposedly 'civilized nation,' and even if we had in-real-time evidence of grave human rights abuses, everyone was too busy celebrating the New Year to care. And, of course, international law did not bring justice to the victims of Operation Cast Lead.

That New Year of 2009, my twenty-eighth birthday, was very different from my thirteenth birthday when I witnessed the Zapatista uprising. Instead, I witnessed the absence of effective solidarity mechanisms. Millions of interconnected citizens were watching and ignoring an atrocity without interrupting their celebrations and acting to stop it accordingly. There were no global leaders marching united then. I wondered, "What will be the thing that will actually make everyone at least stop and see such crimes, and then act to terminate them?" It was clear to me that for the oppressed, to make people really stop, listen and care, new tactics were needed. The Zapatistas achieved that taking the world by surprise on a New Year's eve. But after that, the world went back to its lethargic mode and I kept wondering what will be needed to make people stop and realize what was going on in the world. That was achieved by Wikileaks, when they published the Collateral Murder video.

JF   For the audience, can you just describe a little more about what the Zapatista movement was? How long before WikiLeaks was this?

RA   It was more than a decade before WikiLeaks existed, and only a few years after internet use had become widespread. The web enabled the democratization of the Internet as an open platform for all. The Zapatista Liberation Army, known as the 'EZLN uprising', was a different one. It was an armed occupation led by organised Maya peasants. It combined local and global struggles: it was a reaction against NAFTA, against globalization and the threat to the poor and excluded. However, it was not a purely defensive action; it was also an uprising designed to make the voices of the people of Chiapas heard, to open the possibility of reclaiming control over their occupied territories and resources, and to demand an end to the abuse and discrimination perpetrated by the Mexican Federal State.

The uprising was launched in January 1994 while the municipalities in Chiapas were under-staffed and off-guard due to the New Year's festivities. The Zapatistas, comprised of more than 2,000 indigenous men and women, and armed with rudimentary weapons, took physical control over towns, cities, and rural areas across Chiapas. A force equivalent to no more than a fragment (0.1%) of the Mexican Army was able to successfully resist and to maintain control of a significant part of the state. During the 12 days of the initial uprising, the slogan most heard was: "Enough is Enough!".[9] Autonomous Zapatista territories were organized following the uprising and they still have self-governance to this day, with a parallel system of education, healthcare and even hacker spaces and autonomous communications. This was not achieved in isolation but was assisted by international solidarity. Marcos, in all his attractive anonymity, acted as a kind of fiction in the West, almost a superhero character. He inspired the international popular support that the Zapatistas needed in order to survive. It was also very different from previous popular uprisings because of the Zapatistas' ability to ensure a flow of information from the zone of conflict. They were able to produce real-time, eye-witness reporting that could counter the narrative of

9. The slogan that the Zapatista Rebels have written on their banner is "Basta ya!" or "Enough is Enough!" In their first communiqué, issued on the first day of their uprising, the EZLN states: But today, we say ENOUGH IS ENOUGH. We are the inheritors of the true builders of our nation. The dispossessed, we are millions and we thereby call upon our brothers and sisters to join this struggle as the only path, so that we will not die of hunger due to the insatiable ambition of a 70-year dictatorship led by a clique of traitors that represent the most conservative and sell-out groups.

the state. And this was almost two decades before the Arab Spring, which is so often cited when people discuss the power of the internet in relation to popular struggle. They regained and kept their autonomy and the control they wanted over key institutions.

SH   Controlled by them, you mean?

RA   Yes, by the Zapatistas. Governed by the community as opposed to the ruling party. And education has been transformed into a different model.

JF   Sarah, can you tell us how you became politically active? It's interesting to hear that Renata was planning to study science when I know that you studied science as well.

SH   Yes, the same field as it happens - biochemistry.

RA   So I would have met you anyway.

SH   Renata brought up the technical side as well. It's interesting, the cross-over of concerns that a number of us have in investigative journalism, truth, science, document publication, and, of course, WikiLeaks. I think my path to activism consisted of a gradual realization of what I wanted to do. Since I was very young, in a kind of naïve way, I had always wanted to do 'good' and to help people. But I didn't really know what the best way to realize this desire was in practice. I remember having a lot of conversations with my dad, who was interested in politics, about how to solve various social problems. For example, at a very young age I wrote to the then-Prime Minister of the UK

about an idea I had on how to solve the issue of home-
less people – an eight-year-old's plan to give them jobs and
houses. As I grew up, though, the solutions I encountered
that were out there just did not seem very effective – for
instance solutions proposed by many NGOs and the like.
So I went around doing what I could, and searching for
my real path. I would volunteer with various organizations
and try to feel as if I was doing something useful, but I
never felt these were the best ways of effecting real change
in the world. And, essentially, I went through my formal
education, just doing what I was interested in, and that was
initially science and then literature.

Later, I started on the path to investigative journalism. I was very
specific about the type of journalism I wanted to do. I thought the
only type of journalism that had any real benefit was that which
uncovered truths and gave documented factual information to people about the world around them. I wanted to do journalism that
gave the ordinary people the agency and capacity to pursue change,
rather than doing the kind of reporting that just tells you what the
latest politician was espousing or pontificating on. And then, like
everyone else here, I became involved with WikiLeaks. So, we can all
blame Julian for the fact we are sitting around this table! Or, rather,
we should celebrate him! To me, working at WikiLeaks represented
the culmination of a number of things that I already enjoyed doing. I
felt passionately about their importance. It was an opportunity to use
a number of skills I had cultivated, and all of the work I've done with
WikiLeaks has fit within my ideals. So, for instance, Julian's concept

of "scientific journalism" – using raw data, along with investigative journalism to provide people with facts and documents they can use to empower themselves — actually also relates to a secret dream I had when I was little of being a librarian. Now I am working at WikiLeaks, the coolest library in the world. I have to say, I also love the adrenaline rush that I get from the release of our publications.

WHEN YOU'RE PART OF THE NEWS STORIES THAT ARE BEING WRITTEN, YOU UNDERSTAND WHAT THE TRUTH IS

JF   Before you were politically active, did you ever realize that the information you were being fed through the media was often not actually always the truth, or it wasn't actually founded in fact? Were you ever a passive recipient of the news? You might never have been, but I know I was. I used to read the papers and go "Oh!" And it was only when WikiLeaks emerged that I started to read the news and say to myself, "Oh?".

SH   I suppose it depends what you mean by "passive recipient". There's two ways, I think, in which one could be a passive recipient of the news. In the first instance, you could simply believe everything you're reading. But another way to be a passive recipient is to be more skeptical, but not to actually do anything about it. Very few people actually do something after having learning about injustice through the mainstream media. Few feel empowered enough or are propelled to act. The news is presented to them in a passive a manner that seems to be designed to encourage passive consumption. I didn't always believe everything I read, although I think I've become much more critical now. Having seen the media at close first-hand, and having seen inaccurate stories both from inside and from being a subject of stories – having seen articles that appear in the news about WikiLeaks, and Edward Snowden, and even myself – has made me much more skeptical about mainstream reporting. When you see news that you are actually directly involved in, it's shocking to see how the facts of the matter are not presented correctly; it's spun, and sometimes even outright lies are used. I understand some people just completely passively eat up the news, but there's a lot of people who understand that the media papers do lie to them. But I think I only understood the full extent to which the media deceive us after working at WikiLeaks. I also gained very interesting insight into mainstream notions of truth from an experience I had when I was working on a documentary at the BIJ [Bureau of Investigative Journalism]. I was asked to start to fact-check a script for a Channel 4 news documentary and so I asked my co-workers, "What is your standard for fact-checking?"

JF   How do you actually check the facts?

SH   Yeah. Do we need source documents for every single little thing? Or what's your criteria for deciding if something is true or not? And they said, "Oh, if it's reported by two reputable news organizations it's trustworthy."

AR   God!

SH   So, of course, this raises the question: what is a reputable news organization? It's such a subjective matter. How many lies have the BBC and *The Times*, for example, broadcast or printed? And I'm not just talking about deliberate lies, but also factual inaccuracies – lets give them the benefit of the doubt that the inaccuracies are often unintentional. But then these inaccuracies (or lies) are published, and, as per what I was told for the Channel 4 documentary can then become cemented as "fact" and used as the supporting source for a certain "fact". This then perpetuates the cycle and that narrative is then accepted as the established "truth" by all other media.

I don't think I was necessarily a passive recipient of the news in the sense that I believed everything I read, although I'm much more critical now. But there were many stories I would read and I would think, "But what can I actually do about it?" I felt very detached from the news. And I think one of the beauties of WikiLeaks is that when you have these large databases made available it can break through the public's detachment. Because people can then do their own research, find out information themselves, and write their own stories. In this way, I think WikiLeaks has been really empowering for a great many people. And what we saw in the case of CableGate,[10] which was such a large internationally co-produced publication, was that all of the publicly-initiated sites such as WikiLeaks Central and WikiLeaks Press, and many other people all over the globe started

10. See WikiLeaks' CableGate archive: https://wikileaks.org/plusd/?qproject[]
=cg&q=#result

to get involved and do their own research, using their own expertise, regarding their own localities. All of these initiatives that sprang up around CableGate showed that the public could now access their own history, access the truths that were specific to them, and use that information to combat injustice.

RA   For me, the shift in my view of the media didn't start with CableGate, it began earlier. The Guatemalan media environment is quite compromised and everyone in Guatemala assumes that the media lies. We have fewer and fewer national news sources, so the narrative of national media, with all its corruption and flaws is distributed across international news networks. And domestically, there is little investment in our own media outlets or public media. Before, local productions and news were needed to keep the official narrative during the war, but during peace times, even pro government media declined. There is both scarcity and low quality reporting, domestically.[11]

While I was preparing the evidence of genocide, for the case I mentioned earlier, I was working with different, complementary sets of facts. When you are in a country in conflict[12] you are exposed to different versions of a story constantly, and to public and private accounts of events. I was looking at versions from the national press, from the international press, from witnesses, from perpetrators

---

11.   For more information on Guatemalan media, see 'Mapping Digital Media: Guatemala', *Open Society Foundation*: https://archive.is/1RED2

12.   See 'Timeline: Guatemala's Brutal Civil War', *PBS Newshour*: https://archive.is/5EKkt

avoiding justice, and from survivors who were directly impacted. Additionally, I was looking at evidence from scientific experts, regarding environmental damage, and forensic evidence, as well as evidence from the military chain of command and details regarding the purchases of the military.[13] The most impressive aspect of the work was seeing the remarkable research done by the Guatemalan Forensic Anthropology Association[14] and its ability to contest the narrative of the military and the government when the latter was denying its involvement in atrocities and seeking to obscure the age of genocide victims, the causes of their deaths, and the nature of the human remains found in mass graves. Those who were denying that a genocide ever happened were arguing against scientific facts, against the actual bones buried in secret mass graves that showed the effects of torture and murder. The scale of the genocide was so great that, in fact, it did not take long to uncover the physical evidence.

Even when the powerful attempt to hide the truth, they can never entirely prevent truths emerging. Especially now, as we are getting better and better at developing scientific methods of fact-checking which can actually be used to prosecute genocide.[15] In addition to the greater use of forensic evidence, crimes such as the Guatemalan genocide can be exposed by better on-the-ground

13. See 'Data Mining for Good [30c3]', YouTube: https://archive.is/zJGnR
14. Guatemalan Forensic Anthropology Foundation: https://archive.is/ul73F http://en.wikipedia.org/wiki/Guatemalan_Forensic_Anthropology_Foundation
15. See Patrick Ball, 'Using Data to Prosecute Genocide', YouTube: https://archive.is/1RMdu, and 'The Body Counter', Foreign Policy: https://archive.is/kwqPi

reporting. For instance, I volunteered for a platform called Global Voices Online,[16] which sought to create a community of curators who fostered local conversations and a network of volunteer translators to make those conversations available in different languages.

The "facts" regarding international events, reported from a Eurocentric, remote perspective, are often misleading or even detrimental if one wants to gain an accurate idea of what is going on in the world. Mainstream reporting just provides an incomplete snapshot each time a terrible event happens and emphasizes the importance of certain events and downgrades others. For instance, compare the huge amount of reporting on the Boston Marathon Bombing as compared to the negligible reporting on the constant bombings in Karachi. Furthermore, due to language and cultural barriers, there are often many facts missing from the media portrayal of events in the Global South, often reported by people who do not really know the locality they are reporting from. There are so many incorrect facts reported regarding other non-Western countries, and so many countries that are barely even mentioned in the news. There are certain countries that are just not on the map for Western media outlets. Of course, international media coverage is also constrained by business decisions - for instance, it is more cost effective to send a foreign correspondent to a particular country occasionally, rather than having regular on-the-ground reporting. Furthermore, media organizations are still in love with the idea of exclusivity, and so are reluctant to build partnerships with local outlets.

16. See the Global Voices Manifesto: https://archive.is/FBCYn and 'Global Voices – citizen media stories from around the world': https://archive.is/DDkbf

During the CableGate release, WikiLeaks launched a different strategy of publication. It connected with courageous local outlets in more than 50 countries, distributing the relevant material to them, because WikiLleaks knew that the people on the ground were the ones who could rapidly and effectively localize the news. Knowing the local context and the local complexities produces news that is very different from what the *New York Times* tells you.

SH   And local people can go and find out the facts on the ground, using the connections and abilities that they have.

RA   Thinking about it more carefully, the combination of scientific data and localized interpretation is really important in places like Guatemala and other underreported countries, which are places where very little data is collected and where very limited research is done. For instance, researching the Guatemalan genocide required me to use both the scientific data and localized interpretation, working with around 54 genocide survivors[17] from various communities. That experience really helped to change me from being a passive recipient of the news to being an active seeker of truth.

JF   Angela, when did you start to become a more active participant in politics?

17. For reference, see summary of genocide proceedings: https://v.gd/Rt6Q6e

AR   I was initially quite passive, but for different reasons than for the average Western European. Rather, it was cynicism at some level, because my parents are from Eastern Europe, from the former Yugoslavia, and I was always brought up with the idea that mass media is propaganda. In Yugoslavia it was clear that everybody who was in charge was lying to you. Propaganda was seen as the most natural thing in the world. So I was always aware of media lies. To my surprise, I realized that this was also true in the supposedly free West, but the only difference is that Western propaganda is more sophisticated. And so, at a certain point I just became very cynical and very typically Western in my outlook. I was obsessed with my own life and with feeding my ego. However, living in that way made me really miserable after a while. My own cynicism and narcissism conflicted with my upbringing. At some point I just couldn't ignore the propaganda. Things changed for me during the war in Yugoslavia in the 1990s. I was directly affected by it because of my family background, and the discrepancies in the media reporting were very clear to me. For example, the British reporting of the war was very different from that of the Germans because of their past relationships with the warring parties. The Germans have a Second World War history with the Croatians – the shared ideology and collaboration between the Croatian Ustaše[18] and the Nazis. So they had a different take on the war than the British, who historically were much

closer to Serbia, with whom Britain was allied during
World War One.

Later on, in the mid-2000s, when Julian was just starting to develop
WikiLeaks, I sensed a lot of decadence and narcissism in Western
mainstream media. For example, when the catastrophic nuclear
accident happened in Fukushima it was big news everywhere, but
on the same page as a report on the accident you would find a big
story on Kim Kardashian's buttocks! Well, Fukushima disappeared
from the news, despite the fact that the reactors will continue to emit
radiation for God knows how many years. But Kim Kardashian's
posterior is still a regular fixture in the news. Unfortunately, when
you're an artist you're much more in contact with this narcissistic
part of Western culture.

Personally, I find it difficult to define truth precisely because
truth can't just be found in a document. But a document is maybe
something that can help to prove a fact. And of course a lot of facts
together become something like truth, you can come very close to
truth. But truth is always complex.

JF   And it's subjective too.

SH   Yes. For instance, we could have a disagreement in this
          room, and I could come away thinking it was just an intel-
          lectual conversation that got heated, and you could come

18. Ustaša, also spelled Ustasha, plural Ustaše, was a Croatian fascist move-
    ment that nominally ruled the Independent State of Croatia during World
    War II. Its members murdered hundreds of thousands of Serbs, Jews,
    Roma and anti-fascist or dissident Croats in Yugoslavia during World
    War II.

away thinking we shouted at each other and that it was a really awful experience. How we experience that conversation is completely subjective. WikiLeaks publishes facts, for example the US State Department cables. They aren't necessarily the whole truth about something, but they are important facts. That a cable was written stating X by someone at a certain time is a fact. However, the whole truth about the situation described in the cable will be an amalgamation of what is revealed by the cable, the views of others interested parties, what records aside from the specific cable reveal, and the wider context and history.

THE REAL TEST OF ANY MOVEMENT OR ANY SOCIETY IS ITS TOLERANCE FOR THE PHILOSOPHER

JF   You are all very courageous women. You have different backgrounds, but you have one thing in common, which is that you are both courageous and also practical, and so you are able to use your courage to really effect change. WikiLeaks has created significant change in the power dynamics of journalism. But how do you as practical, courageous women envisage maintaining and growing this movement and making it sustainable for the long term?

RA   In my case, I have been involved in many of the interlinked battles that have led to this quite singular movement. With the arrival of the internet, new battles between ordinary people and the powerful have emerged. For example, the battle for preservation of privacy, anonymity, and the struggle to make knowledge open and accessible for everyone. The access-to-knowledge battle has created the potential basis for a movement, which now includes a broad group of actors, from librarians to radical investigative journalists, from activists fighting against the TPP[19] to musicians

---

19.   Trans-Pacific Partnership, the largest-ever economic treaty, encompassing 12 nations and representing more than 40% of the world's GDP: https://archive.is/d9uAS

exploring new forms of production outside of copyright. So, there are organized groups with related struggles that might lead to the creation of a quite powerful movement.

I think we already have the basic ingredients, which combined, might lead us to the creation of a movement. We have dispersed groups of engaged individuals that have very different political perspectives and that have very divergent points of interest. And these groups are very marginal in the information ecosystem. If you compare our movement to the environmental movement, we are still at the very early stage and we are not developing quickly enough. And we are losing. We had in our hands this incredibly powerful tool that was open to everyone, and that enabled creation, disruption, and action. Yet that same tool is being used by our opponents to gain total control over us.

SH   That tool being the internet?

RA   Yes, and new technologies that could have operated as decentralized platforms of liberation, as opposed to what are public-private partnerships of control and oppression.

AR   At the risk of sounding paranoid, I think that we're facing the threat of a real transnational totalitarianism. It may sound like a conspiracy theory, but the Snowden leaks[20] revealed the merging of intelligence agencies with private

20. To search the documents disclosed by Edward Snowden and read media articles written about them, see the 'Revelations' section of the Free Snowden website: https://edwardsnowden.com/revelations/ and searchable archive at: https://search.edwardsnowden.com/

tech companies and the military industrial complex. The entity formed from these parts is growing uncontrollably, like a cancer, collecting vast amounts of data as well as resources, and massively reducing privacy. That entity is growing out of all proportion and may well kill its host, like a kind of monstrous parasite. The capabilities of mass surveillance are a severe threat to free societies and democracy. And it goes far beyond traditional US imperialism. All this is very precisely documented in the book *Cypherpunks*.[21] When the book was first published in Germany, many critics described its viewpoint as skewed and paranoid. And then, one year later, Snowden came forward with his revelations about the NSA, and the thesis propounded in *Cypherpunks* was revealed to be absolutely true.

AR   It seems like a real David against Goliath struggle, but there is a chance we can win.

RA   If we need to reduce the aims of the movement to one goal, I would say it would be to preserve freedom of thought. And for that, to have real freedom of thought, you have to eradicate surveillance. You have to preserve freedom of expression. You have to enable access to knowledge, fight censorship, and also enable creation. Because how can you have freedom of thought if you are just passive recipients? So, from my perspective, that would be the goal. And it is

21. Assange Julian; Appelbaum Jacob; Müller-Maguhn Andy; Zimmermann Jérémie: *Cypherpunks: Freedom and the Future of the Internet*, New York 2012.

really tricky to make it happen because many people are not aware of their rights, and furthermore, this emerging totalitarian state that you describe so well is very tempting and appealing to people in some respects.

AR   For the privileged.

RA   Not just the privileged. For instance, consider someone who has connected to the internet for the first time, in a Guatemalan village say. Because they cannot afford the Super-Plus plan on their little mobile phone that would give them "full access to Internet, without restrictions or filters" they instead have only Facebook, a platform controlled by a private company whose sole real interest is profit and market share. And as a result they will have a poor Internet for poor people, which will only extract their data. It will offer a limited space for creation, it will place them at greater risk of surveillance, monitoring and discrimination. That is the idea the mainstream promotes as "access". Obviously, this will very significantly alter the kind of content that people in the global South have access to. It is rather like having access to a poorly constructed road where it will take you longer to reach your destination, or to a building that is outside a gated community. Your freedom is circumscribed by poverty. An internet

22. Net neutrality requires that the internet be maintained as an open platform, on which network providers treat all content, applications and services equally, without discrimination.

without net neutrality[22] simply replicates structures of inequality and exclusion. However, one must not lose perspective. It makes me angry how relative the reactions of people are – how global leaders react with "concern" when a website is blocked, but how shy their reaction is when the abuses exposed are torture or extrajudicial killings. If the internet is blocked in Turkey, everyone makes a big fuss. If five people are tortured in Turkey, no one cares.

JF   So you're saying that we need to maintain a free internet.

RA   I would say that preserving an open and free internet might be a battle we are arriving at too late and is one that we might well lose. Maybe we have lost already, and the only option we have is to take to the trenches to preserve whatever is left of our civil liberties. We might be only able to defend a small degree of the possibilities we once had to connect and organize with others, and to circulate information and ideas.

SH   I would offer a single word that I believe potentially sums up the goal for this movement, and that is "self-determination". The ability for ordinary people to determine their own lives is crucial. Whether that's online or whether it's a journalist being able to report what they want, or whether it's a country being able to decide for itself what its laws should be. I think all these questions come down to an individuals' ability to exercise self-determination. WikiLeaks is such an important force in this movement because self-determination is one of its main goals. The very way in which it operates aids self-determination. The documents and archives WikiLleaks publishes, allow any member of the public to gain a greater understanding of the world around them, and to utilize the documents to try to effect change however they wish.

So protecting WikiLeaks is so important, because the documents published by it have aided the struggle for self-determination on so many occasions. For example, in 2003 Khalid El-Masri,[23] a German citizen, was abducted while on holiday in Macedonia and then rendered to a secret CIA prison in Afghanistan, where he was tortured by his captors. He was later released, dumped in Albania, and spent years unsuccessfully trying to get justice. When WikiLeaks published cables about his case, including evidence that US officials had pressured German officials, El-Masri and his legal team were able to use those cables at the European Court of Human Rights, which cited the WikiLeaks documents in its judgement.[24] And so we can see that when people have the ability to access documents, their own historical record, the possibilities for change and the achievement of justice go far beyond that of mere journalism.

---

23. See Khalid El-Masri Wikipedia page: https://archive.is/1aGuu
24. See 'Khaled el-Masri: German citizen, innocent victim of CIA rendition and torture', WikiLeaks Press: https://archive.is/25KSi, and El-Masri v the Former Yugoslav Republic of Macedonia judgment: https://archive.is/x4R8K

THE ASSUMPTION THAT GLENN GREENWALD AND LAURA POITRAS ARE MORE INTELLIGENT THAN ME...

JF   Recently in the United Kingdom, we've seen the *Guardian* reporting on the Snowden revelations. Everybody's been very upset about the revelations of NSA surveillance. And then the British government responded by introducing the UK IP Bill[25] that will enormously increase the powers of surveillance in the UK. So, in spite of all the excitement around the Snowden revelations, including amongst not especially radical average *Guardian* readers, it looks like we're just going backwards on the surveillance front.

SH   There was a story regarding the NSA revelations, by Glenn Greenwald at *The Intercept*,[26] about how the FBI and NSA had been spying on people – racially profiling them – by monitoring their email accounts. The article detailed the stories of just five individuals, even though the list of people being spied on ran to many thousands. The details regarding the thousands of others were simply redacted. Not

25.   See 'UK IP Bill is a threat to privacy, security, and trust online', Open Policy & Advocacy: https://archive.is/4B8Nq
26.   See 'Meet the Muslim-American Leaders the FBI and NSA Have Been Spying On', *The Intercept*: https://archive.is/NSqGB

long after it was published I looked at all the readers' comments on the article, and there were quite a number from people demanding to know if their own email addresses were on the list. Some commenters called for the entire list to be published and some people even stated their email addresses, and asked the authors if their email addresses were included on the list. Hardly any of the commenters said that they would prefer their address to not be published if, in fact, their email address was on the list. In fact, one commenter even asked, "How does one find out if one's name is on the surveillance list? Through WikiLeaks?"

So this is one example of many that shows that people do actually want this information. They want to be able to use it to protect themselves and gain a better understandinging of their world. The power imbalance is such that governments and intelligence services, thousands and thousands of people, have access to all our information, and we barely know about it. The very people and institutions that have been shown to be unable to protect our rights, who are in fact violating them, have all the power. The only way to improve the situation is to publish such information without redaction. It's far better that everyone has access to this information than just the corrupt elite.

WikiLeaks publishes complete archives, but we have seen that many of the beneficial effects one might have expected actually have been blocked because of the mainstream media's strategy of publishing the material with heavy redactions. I think WikiLeaks is so important, because it sets an example by publishing complete, unreacted material. It is the only example that I can think of right now of an organization that publishes entire suppressed archives on a massive, global scale.

JF   Can you imagine such material being used in a future Truth Commission?

SH   Exactly. Yes, the concept of working with source documents in this way, to uncover the truth is similar to the concept of the Truth Commission. Earlier, Joseph, you were talking about the NSA example. In my opinion the journalists working on the NSA stories are setting a very different example from the one set by WikiLeaks. The documents are coming out, but they're being published with heavy redactions. And I think actually they've taken a step back from the example that we fought so hard to set, which is really quite sad. These journalists are assuming that the public needs a journalistic filter on information to which we are all entitled to have access. They even seem to be celebrating the fact that they redact the material they receive.

RA   Well, information is power and they want to keep that power in the hands of journalists. They don't mind seeing agency stripped from the people.

SH   And right now the powerful are able to win, because there is such a disparity between their access to knowledge and the access that ordinary people have. The powerful succeed because in our society it is only those that have become powerful that are able to exercise real self-determination.

I actually don't wish to concentrate on stopping powerful people from holding the positions that they currently occupy. But rather to even up the balance of knowledge so that every Joe on the street has the power to exercise self-determination. And maybe occupying positions of power, just won't allow people to dominate others in the way that they are currently able.

JF   That reminds me of what Renata said earlier. It's about letting people know what their rights are.

RA   Our right to access knowledge is really under threat. It's not only under threat because of attacks on the press and because of suppression of information, but due to the international architecture that is forming now, under the TPP and other factors. For example, there are the copyright lobbyists in Hollywood, who play a central part in blocking our access to information. Then there are governments such as the Chinese and the Russian who are putting up information walls that are impeding their citizens' access to knowledge. And then there are governments who use poverty as a weapon to keep their citizens marginalized. Of course, people in the latter situation have very limited access to the information that WikiLleaks has been able to disclose. When we discuss the difference between the WikiLeaks revelations versus the NSA revelations, I'm always aware that many people don't have access to either. And so for me, despite the unprecedented effort of WikiLeaks to make knowledge accessible by collaborating with local partners, it's still not enough. We're still reaching a very limited number of countries and contexts. The person that really comes to my mind when we discuss this topic is Aaron Swartz, one of the thought leaders of free culture, an activist who understood the power of knowledge and information in the hands of people.[27]

AR   I was just about to mention him.

RA   And not only Aaron Swartz, but all these other activists in Africa, Latin America, and India that are trying to make knowledge accessible for all people. Bassel Khartabil[28] in Syria, Alaa Abd El-Fattah[29] in Egypt are two examples of activists doing great work in this area. With regard to such activists I also find myself thinking about the way the system is organized in such a way that it filters out such individuals and only certain people are able to get to become the real decision-makers at the top.

AR   I think Aaron Swartz was clearly ahead of his time. His radical way of seeing things was really new in history: he uncompromisingly demanded that everybody should have unlimited and free access to knowledge. Defining who has the right to access knowledge has always been a weapon in the arsenal of the ruling class. And knowledge was never granted for free. I mean, most of you are

27. See Aaron Swartz Wikipedia page: https://archive.is/3yCKC and 'The Internet's Own Boy: The Story of Aaron Swartz': https://archive.is/PRiIS
28. See Bassel Khartabil Wikipedia page: https://archive.is/gk1ze
29. See Alaa Abd El-Fattah Wikipedia page: https://archive.is/qfUij

from Anglo-Saxon countries; here in Germany it's better, because we largely don't have to pay for education, but in the United States and the United Kingdom further education is hugely expensive. However, as the new tools and technology to access knowledge become more easily available, there is at least the possibility of challenging the old education system. It was that struggle that Aaron Swartz was engaged in.

RA It's a more participatory culture. Unlike in earlier eras, the user can actually become the creator, and technology allows for the proliferation decentralized non-hierarchical organization. If I was to describe what is the most important objective in this war that we are fighting, it is that we should insist that access to knowledge and the possibilities that it brings cannot be limited to the few.

JF OK. So that brings me back to your question: why do you think the NSA revelations have actually seen our struggle move backwards?

SH When you talk about the NSA revelations, you're talking about documents created by the United States. The United States is a hugely powerful imperialist country that exercises influence over most other states. What the United States government does has big consequences for people and states all over the world. And so, I would argue, that the information that the US government creates should be accessible to all of the people that it affects. In fact, in many cases, the data and documents are created from information that actually already belongs to the victims of surveillance. What you have though, in the case of the NSA disclosures is that a very small number of people are now in control of the information and are themselves deciding what the public should know. They have actually categorically said that the whole archive won't be coming out. Not only will the information be published at a ridiculously slow rate (and all full of redactions), but also they have actually stated on several occasions that much of the material won't be published at all. So information that I believe everybody has the right to access is never going to come into the public domain, because of journalists' decisions, and the fact that they are working in collaboration with the US government regarding what they decide to publish.

And what really annoys me, and this is why I think a backwards step has been taken, is that this comes after all the great work WikiLleaks did in 2010, and all the battles we had to counter, including the lies of the US government when they claimed that we had endangered people's lives by releasing information that actually exposed the blood on the hands of the US government. In spite of all the defamatory material coming from the US government and its supporters we still survived, we continued to release information, and we provided a real example of what could be achieved. We successfully demonstrated that the information we published rightfully belonged to everyone. We showed the world it is possible to do this, In spite of government threats and propaganda. And what was key to this was that we didn't keep secrets from the public. Of course, we had battles with our mainstream media partners about that, but the example we successfully set was to publish full archives and that was the principle that our supporters rallied around. We gave examples from our work that demonstrated why this was the right thing to do, and we repudiated the idea that "information is dangerous." There are simply no examples to show that CableGate harmed anyone.

But now we have a situation where journalists such as Glenn Greenwald are portrayed as 'good' journalists, even though they are denying the public information that rightly belongs to all of us. These journalists have reinstated the notion that information is dangerous, an idea that we worked so hard to successfully counter. They have actually managed to make a virtue out of censoring information. They are celebrated for their "responsibility" and yet nobody asks to whom they are responsible. They have reversed the great gains that WikiLeaks had made for freedom of expression by saying: "We are good journalists because we are listening to the government, and redacting information, for reasons we can't tell you." Rather than saying, as we did: "These are your documents, your history. Information itself doesn't harm."

RA   It seems that the publication of the NSA documents and those from other intelligence agencies was done at a very different pace and style from WikiLeaks' publications.

SH   With the way the publication is happening?

RA   Yes, I understand that it is a very complex set of documents that requires a level of technical expertise which very few people in the world have. So in the case of the

NSA revelations we have seen people from a technical background effectively becoming journalists. I'm thinking of people like Jacob Appelbaum, Bruce Schneier and Andy Muller-Maghun. They've taken on the journalistic responsibility of trying to make the information accessible to ordinary people. It's understandable that few people have the specialized knowledge to do this kind of work, which has always been quite inaccessible for the general public. But the pace of the NSA publications is extremely slow and predominantly in English.[30] Most of the time it's focused on EU and US countries, with very little participation by journalists from other countries, and all the documents are heavily redacted. This adds further complexity for independent experts who might be able to interpret the information differently. Again, the local and the scientific elements that I mentioned earlier when discussing fact-checking, are missing, so I would like more people to be able to see the full technical documents.

SH   It's very difficult, if not impossible in many cases, to use these documents in a legal case, because they are so incomplete.

RA   And that is especially relevant due to the nature of the documents and the architecture safeguarding the secrecy of NSA data. There are no alternatives ways to find the

30. Journalist Joshua Eaton of *Al-Jazeera America* created a timeline of the most relevant NSA-related publications: https://archive.is/HCkrJ. A useful comparison can be made withWikiLeaks' media partners for CableGate: https://archive.is/esURA

information. For instance, Freedom of Information requests are futile - they are systematically denied on national security grounds.

SH   And with just one page of a 20-page document it's impossible to make a legal case.

RA   I'm bothered by this assumption that Glenn Greenwald and Laura Poitras will know better than ordinary people and that we all have to blindly trust their journalistic judgement. I have a lot of respect for Greenwald's journalism, especially his opinion pieces, and Laura is an award winning filmmaker. But I wish they would let us see more than just fragments of the NSA documents. And I can only think about those who are targeted by the US military, those whose names are on these "kill lists". Will those names ever be revealed? I have to question whether these journalists understand the global and local context of these revelations well enough to decide what should and shouldn't be published. Furthermore, will we ever know what they decided not to publish, and what they decided to redact? Will we ever find out how they came to trust the government's advice regarding omissions and redactions?

I am also realistic and I understand that publishing the documents in their entirety will require stronger safeguards and protection for journalists, publications, sources and their families. Great care needs to be taken regarding the personal data of those who are at risk of being targeted by the powerful. So we need to get better at what we are doing. We need new business models, new legal frameworks that allow journalists to publish freely, without checking with the government first, and a new ethical framework. Sadly, instead of being able to push for such reforms, we have drifted back to the pre-WikiLeaks era.

JF   So we're seeing a reversion to traditional journalism?

SH   Yes, but now done in such a way that journalists such as Glenn Greenwald are actually celebrated for publishing redacted material. The public is actively encouraged to commend journalists for telling them less, for keeping information from them. The work of such journalists is superficially similar to WikiLeaks and consciously imitates the style of WikiLeaks publications. For that reason, the public fails to see it for what it really is.

RA   If you look at media today, it is monopolistic, corrupt, non-transparent, and effectively captured by governments and corporations. Potentially the publication of complete, unredacted documents might act to at least make visible the capture of the media by powerful interests. But, at the same time, I am very aware of the economic and political constraints. The current setup, where only journalists can see full documents, feels similar to many religions, where only a certain class had access to knowledge.

AR   That's what I meant when I said it was too early to expect people to think for themselves and gain confidence in their own judgement. People are very used to being patronized and lectured by approved 'professionals' and it is actually very comfortable to be told what to think, and not to have to exercise any responsibility.

RA   WikiLeaks challenged the reader to directly access the source documents, as Sarah explained earlier. That changed the game. WikiLeaks used to publish without intermediaries, which is what made the release of the Collateral Murder video so powerful. For a period of time WikiLeaks made partnerships with mainstream Western media organizations. But more recently, its role as custodian of the repository of all information risking suppression has increased, with the creation of an advanced and stable interface[31] that allows anyone to find relevant source documents. When WikiLeaks opened the archive to everyone, really interesting stuff started to emerge from those archives. Perhaps it is naïve, but I still feel discriminated against when I read the global headlines every morning. Countries from the global South are never a priority. Tragedies or important issues affecting those countries never capture the attention of the world. The reporting about the NSA has been no exception to this rule and, unsurprisingly, advocacy for surveillance reform has followed that trend as well. The rights of European and American citizens are at the center of these reform efforts. Equality across borders is the missing ingredient, both in the reporting and the policy debate. No NGO has put forward the equality of the human right to privacy regardless of one's nationality.

31.   See WikiLeaks' Advanced Search interface: https://search.wikileaks.org/advanced?q=&page=

SH   Have you seen the color of your skin?

RA   Yes, I'm very aware of that, especially in this room. It is interesting to see how protecting themselves from surveillance is really a matter of life and death for many people in the global south. In many countries of the global south surveillance is used as a tool to target and kill. By not informing such people of the dangers they face, the journalists who decide not to share certain information are...

JF   Destroying self-determination.

RA   Exactly.

JF   You're talking about things being redacted?

RA   No, no, no! I'm talking about the decisions and prioritizing regarding what actually gets released - not the redactions. If these journalists choose not to release certain documents, they are denying people in the south the access they need for survival. And, of course, there's not a big global outcry over this issue, partly because of the war on terror narrative, but also people in the global north are sufficiently distanced from the issue that they see it as disconnected from their own daily struggles.

SH   Half the world has no idea about this issue.

RA   At the end of the day, journalism is all about power and control. It is very problematic that there are vast amounts of documents still unpublished and that the pace of release is so slow. Moreover, the NSA and other agencies, their accomplices in the surveillance business, have now had more than a year and a half to prepare themselves in order to develop their counter narratives, hide the evidence of their wrongdoing and find ways to keep the surveillance machinery working.

The NSA revelations are reported from the USA, Germany and a few other countries and all of the reporting is directed by American journalists who are subject to, and influenced by, the laws and standards of the USA. They are openly consulting with and working together with their own governments. Collaborating with governments will of course, not simply protect people susceptible to harm but will also lead to the protection of special interests who want to avoid scrutiny. For example, the US-led War on Drugs is a case where a lot of 'sensitive' information is yet to be released. We have heard very little about what is going on with the War on Drugs in Latin America with regard to surveillance. Maybe the Snowden documents have very little information about it, who knows? But, with millions of documents pending publication, it is reasonable that journalists will wonder and seek access to those documents because, for Latin America, there is the possibility that there is significant material on the War on Drugs in the NSA documents. If the documents had been published in their entirety we could easily find out, but, instead, we are still awaiting publication.

JF   The US government would disagree of course.

RA   Of course, the government wants to keep it secret. Many governments in Latin America also want to keep these documents secret. And, because of government pressure, the journalists who have access to this data might think that it's too dangerous to release such information. The War on Drugs clearly has nothing to do with the public interest of Latin American nations. DEA[32] covert operations are just compounding the Cold War legacy of violence and death in Central America. One has to wonder whether keeping such operations secret is simply serving to increase the corruption, and hide the incompetence, of certain military officers. Secrecy is the best friend of corruption, incompetence, and the waste of public resources. The US donates surveillance equipment to Central American countries as part of the War on Drugs. For fragile or failed states, the possibilities for civil society to fight against the abuse of surveillance powers are even more limited because of US assistance. Potentially the unreleased NSA documents could help us to better understand the surveillance capabilities of Central American countries and how those who are the targets of such surveillance protect themselves.

32.   Drug Enforcement Administration (DEA) is a United States federal law enforcement agency under the US Department of Justice, tasked with combating drug smuggling and use within the United States.

I WISH THAT GOOGLE GOVERNED THE
WORLD INSTEAD OF POLITICIANS

RA   At this moment, I am actually rather scared of the idea of the evolution of the state, and its increasing enmeshment with big tech corporations. I heard a misinformed, reckless and very scary comment from a local politician from a Guatemalan village, who said that: "I wish that Google governed the world instead of politicians."

AR   So we should have "Googlement" instead of "government"?

RA   That may be a good joke, but also a scary one too.

JF   Doesn't Google do that anyway?

AR   I think it's obvious how dominant Google has become. They're everywhere, and they're monitoring everything. They're not only replacing government, they seem to almost have replaced God Almighty himself. In the beginning Google started with an algorithm that would automatically improve itself the more data you gave it – this very simple sort of equation for the foundations of artificial intelligence. Google's apparent omnipotence today is based on this infinite appetite of its constantly learning, all-devouring machine.

RA   A super-powerful corporation doing things more efficiently than many nation states.

AR   Yes, and unlike most nation states, Google is capable of very rapid learning and self-enhancement.

RA   Another example of this is Facebook's creation of 'Facebook Zero'.[33]

JF   What?

RA   'Zero', that's a very scary program.

JF   Is that a 'lite' version? Like a diet version?

RA   Using communication satellites, Facebook Zero freely provides a 'basic' internet service via mobile phones to under-served areas, for example to some remote areas in Africa. Potentially, this will allow Facebook to get virtually everyone to use its platform and will give it access to all of the data of the global poor, in addition to all the data of the richer nations.

AR   Great!

JF   Can you explain why that's a problem? I know why it's a problem, but could you explain in more detail? So, Facebook gives internet access to everyone in Africa, even in remote areas where WiFi is non-existent. Why is this a bad thing?

33. See Facebook Free Basics (formerly Facebook Zero): https://archive.is/zTUMc. See also Project Loon from Google: *https://archive.is/tf9gs* and Internet.org: *https://archive.is/PV7U7*

RA   It's a problem of control, basically, and commodification of the user. For Facebook, the global poor are just a marketing opportunity. Even if you cannot pay for internet access, it is profitable for Facebook to give you access because of the data you will generate. There is nothing altruistic about Facebook's provision of "free" internet.

Facebook Zero does not provide full access to the internet, but, instead, it is giving people access solely to Facebook on phones via a stripped-down text-only version of its mobile website. It is a way to get people hooked into the platform in places where it's not profitable to provide people with access, or where people cannot afford to pay for internet use. So in such places Facebook will arrive and invite everyone to create a profile with their real name and real-time location, with a profile picture. What Facebook has discovered is that free access to the network via their platform is actually the most efficient way to create a massive biometric database – well beyond the capabilities of any government. Effectively Facebook is a private biometric database of all your users, which provides Facebook with a detailed account of their users' actions, personal connections, political opinions, and their cultural tastes.[34]

SH   And emotions too.

RA   Indeed, we have learnt that Facebook secretly altered user's news feeds in order to manipulate their emotions and

34. Facebook Zero was followed by Google Free Zone, which then evolved into Internet.org and Project Loon respectively.

views.[35] It's really rather like keeping a chicken locked in the farmyard shed. Users are engaged in this endless cycle of consumption, whilst unaware that all information that is hosted on Facebook has been completely privatized. Once you violate Facebook's terms of service, you can simply be kicked off the platform. Both users, and all information on Facebook, can be removed at the whim of the company. Facebook holds the power to permanently delete any and all information that the individual user has shared. We have also seen that, for example, Facebook has protected hate speech against Palestinians[36] and engaged in many acts of censorship on many other occasions.[37]

SH   There actually have been some very small positive changes. Not necessarily especially consequential changes per se, but it shows the potential start of a trend. And that is in cases where tech companies experienced pushback from their consumer base that forced them to change their behavior. A good example of this is Vodafone's transparency report.[38] I'm not by any means saying that these small

35. Experimental evidence of massive-scale emotional contagion through social networks Adam Kramer. vol. 111 no. 24, 8788-8790: https://archive.is/FAyQg

36. Dalia Othman, "As Rockets Rain on Gaza, Facebook Does Nothing to Stop Hate Speech Against Palestinians". Global Voices Advox: https://archive.is/Erbu2

37. See, for example, online censorship.org: https://archive.is/5aThf

38. See 'Law Enforcement Disclosure Report', Vodafone: https://archive.is/hbuo4

actions have fixed anything, but it's an example of how companies can be forced to change their behavior with sufficient pressure from below. You don't necessarily need to raise money to defend your interests, you can just show to these companies that they will be hurt in the market unless they adhere to the ethics and laws that are dominant within our society.

Having said that, I don't think the solutions lie in politics, policy, or the corporations. I think the solutions will come from independent tech communities inventing free software that ordinary people can use to protect themselves. We clearly can't rely on states to protect us; we need to create tools that will help us to protect ourselves. Sadly, so far, there have been very few technical details published from the Snowden archive that might provide the tech community with enough information to properly and efficiently counter surveillance and make existing encryption tools more secure.

RA   I think that's where the state becomes relevant, and where decentralization, autonomy, and the question of digital sovereignty, comes into play. It's not just about how many resources you put into developing new technologies. What is important are the decisions you take as a collective and how you design public policies around access, software, and hardware. And it is about sovereignty (and the degree of dependence on external actors) and the role that technology plays in building and maintaining that sovereignty.

Another very important issue that our movement needs to think about is literacy and getting kids to engage in this culture of technological creativity. I have a lot of respect for the struggles of the free software movement, free content plays such an important role. It's really vital for people in the global South to create and distribute their own content, ideas, and cultural expression. All these children that are learning how to code, doing their own stuff, that's Aaron Swartz, that's Julian Assange.

I DO NOT RESPECT ANYONE WHO HAS NOT
BEEN IN PRISON

JF   With regards to Western political dissidents, why do you
think there are there so few women locked up in prison for
dissent?

AR   Because they are cunning. (all laughing)

RA   Beyond just gender, llistening to the views of marginal
groups of our society is also very important. During the
'Stop Watching Us' rally in Washington DC.[39] I found
that the most convincing arguments I heard were coming
from people from minority backgrounds: from the Mus-
lim, Black, and Latino communities. That should show us
where real dissent comes from. Real dissent comes from
the marginalized. Unfortunately, the privileged middle
class is just too comfortable and too distracted to engage
in serious dissent. Yet typically, it's only when middle class
people are especially shocked, or caught up in an instance
of the abuse of power, that such stories will manage to
break into the mainstream.

39. A protest rally against NSA mass surveillance held in Washington DC on
25 October 2013 in the wake of the disclosures by Edward Snowden. See
the Stop Watching Us website: https://archive.is/DR4se

For instance, we can see this in the different media treatment of Aaron Swartz versus the case of my friend Bassel Khartabil in Syria. They were both engaged in the struggle to facilitate open access to information at the global level. One is a Palestinian living in Syria and the other was a guy from a middle-class family, working and living in San Francisco and Cambridge, Massachusetts. Both belonged to the same communities, engaged in exactly the same issues, and knew the same circle of people. The case of Aaron Swartz became mainstream news when he committed suicide and there was a detailed investigation of his persecution by the US judiciary and prosecutors. On the other hand, Bassel[40] has been in prison since 15 March 2012 with little media interest. Before his arrest, he was engaged in the struggle to connect Syria to our movement for free knowledge, and in opening a hackerspace and creating a community around new forms of expression that merge new technology, arts, culture, politics and expression.

JF   Renata, how do you explain the disparity in treatment of the two cases??

RA   It is like when a tragedy is reported: 400 dead in an accident and all the media focus is on the two dead Americans.

SH   I would suggest that there are two aspects to this issue. Firstly, Western media has become much more pervasive around the world. And so the priorities of Western media come to dominate global news coverage. I think also that censorship and repression of free speech is often far more

40. See Freebassel.org: https://archive.is/yeOyz

brutal outside the West. For example, I recently was on a panel with a guy who runs an Egyptian TV show that had been censored by the Egyptian government. In contrast to the Western panelists the Egyptian man (all other panelists were from the West) said: "Well, obviously I am against my TV show being censored, but I look out on the street and there are people dying, and people being shot for political reasons all the time, in a way that isn't so prevalent in the West." The sorts of issues faced by people in such countries are very different from problems of censorship in the West. This was an upper middle-class guy whose TV show was censored. But he is in a country where if a politician dislikes a tweet someone sends, that person might be shot. His point was that he had far bigger things to worry about than whether Facebook was secretly manipulating his emotions. I think that when you have this level of open brutality, a situation where people are struggling to survive in a much more obvious way, the need for dissent and the need for gathering on the streets to fight for collective ideas and basic human rights is much greater. I think that's what explains the difference between the Arab Spring and the Occupy movement, for example.

So, to go back to the question of your Syrian friend and Aaron Swartz I think that there's real prejudice against non-Western countries. Society as a whole just doesn't care, dissidents outside of the West are seen as unimportant 'brown people'. Sadly I think a lot of people do think like that. I think also that from a Western perspective people think that the violence and repression that happens abroad is just, "what happens over there."

RA   Exactly. It's the normalization of brutality in certain contexts.

SH   Yes, and also the greater degree of public protest and opposition is also seen as specific to poorer nations.

RA   Not always.

JF   Angela, you mentioned that your father was a political dissident.

AR   Yes, and I've been thinking about the differences between the Eastern European dissidents of the Cold War era and Western dissidents today. It became clear to me, that the 'Western dissidents' – or let's call them 'digital dissidents' – like Assange and Snowden, but also Jeremy Hammond and Barrett Brown – are not even described as dissidents in the mainstream. Because to admit that we, in the supposedly "free" West, have political prisoners, imprisoned for simply telling the truth, would be a threat to the very idea we have of ourselves as the 'free world'. It is striking that the story of Aaron Swartz only became known to a wider public after his tragic death.

When we compare the case of Western dissidents to those in the east, Pussy Riot in Russia or Ai Wei Wei in China, what is the difference? In German there is a term to describe countries like Russia or China: 'Schurkenstaaten', which could be translated as 'rogue states'.

All of my artistic colleagues in the West enthusiastically supported the members of Pussy Riot imprisoned by the Russian state.[41] *Der Spiegel* magazine published an article about them when they were jailed, and everybody I know in Germany, whether part of the mainstream, or the artistic underground scene, was on their side. Straightaway, around 50 artists signed a petition calling for their immediate release. And I'm sure most of the artists who supported them so eagerly had no idea what the members of the group even represented. I was thinking, "How fascinating, that they all stand up without a trace of doubt and without knowing what Pussy Riot even is." It seemed to me that their reaction was triggered by a combination of liking Pussy Riot's punk attitude, which they're very familiar with, and by hatred of Vladimir Putin, which comes very naturally to people in the West. Yet, at the same time as this huge uproar and show of solidarity regarding Pussy Riot, there are people like Jeremy Hammond sitting in jail for 10 years. Or Julian Assange trapped indefinitely in the Ecuadorian embassy.

Hardly anyone even dares to question these things critically in public. And it's not only a problem confined to the mainstream media. I find this also in debates with people I know. I think there's a resistance to acknowledging that people like Assange are dissidents, because once that's admitted, you would have to conclude that we are living in totalitarian states. This is something which people who

41. A Russian feminist punk rock protest group based in Moscow. In August 2012, two members of the group were sentenced to two years' imprisonment for 'hooliganism based on religious hatred' for performing A Punk Prayer in Moscow's Cathedral of Christ the Saviour. See: https://archive.is/GYpfM

live in the West are afraid to face. And why should they, as long as they are not personally endangered? In many ways, we do have more individual freedom than in the past. For example the situation of women, regarding their societal role, and the scale of gendered oppression has improved a lot. Yet ironically women's expanded freedom is now used to propagate the ideology of Western superiority. The widespread acceptance of homosexuality and feminism in the West is regularly used as a tool in Western propaganda, not to the advantage of oppressed women and homosexuals but rather for demonizing enemies abroad.

SH   We can see the disparity in treatment of Eastern and Western dissidents in the case of Edward Snowden. It's frequently denied that the question of or not what he did was a political act, and that whether he's therefore a political refugee. The US government has instead tried very hard to portray him as a criminal fugitive. His act was inherently political, and he would clearly not receive a fair trial in the US, as we have seen from cases like Manning and Thomas Drake. I think this all relates back to what Angela was saying: the West doesn't want to see it that way. The media just isn't interested in repression of Western dissidents. And politicians don't want to foster a kind of self-reflection regarding their own countries. It's this state of denial and hypocrisy in the West that really enrages me.

AR   Yes, I agree. And ignoring such repression is a way for many people in the West to maintain their own personal freedom and privileges. It's much easier for people in the West to say, "Oh, I just don't see any repression" because then they can do whatever they want, to a certain degree. And by taking such a view you then don't *feel* oppressed. It's what I call a very sophisticated form of totalitarianism.

RA   Yes, and you can be a decent father, a good husband, do your job, because work has been compartmentalized in such a sophisticated, complex way. So you end up engaged in this tiny little aspect of a larger system. So for instance, you might be doing work that would either enable researchers to find a cure for cancer, or enable researchers to find the most effective way to kill people with drugs. In that situation you don't see the connection between your own work and its broader impact. You don't see the connection between your actions, and their effects becomes so blurred that you don't really take responsibility for your own actions anymore.

AR   It's also very easy for the reputations of Western dissidents to be destroyed. You can very quickly be made a pariah by the Western media, as happened to Julian Assange. Truth-tellers are troublemakers, people who threaten a more comfortable lifestyle. Such people who say: "there is something terribly wrong in this country." And indeed something is going terribly wrong in this kind of society; it's a new kind of totalitarianism. I feel very cynical about it when, every day, we see refugees risk their lives to enter Europe in an attempt to be part of this false promise.

JF   Renata, you spoke about the normalization of brutality in various countries, and the different treatment by the media of violence in the East versus violence in the West. So, violence in Syria, is considered normal - because that's just what happens in foreign countries. But why doesn't anyone raise an eyebrow when Chelsea Manning is being tortured in the West?

RA   I would say that brutality has been normalized everywhere.

AR   I think that people in the West don't really believe that people like Chelsea Manning are being tortured. And there is very little reporting on the subject in the media.

AR   That's what I think.

RA   When I was trying to figure out why people don't do anything in response to instances of massive violence and brutality I was reminded of what Mother Teresa once said: "If I look at the mass I will never act. If I look at the one, I will." I think there's a profound truth to that statement. I read something very interesting written by a psychologist,[42] who suggests that people can relate to concrete, real human stories, about people that you can name and who are in situations familiar to yourself. In that case it's relatively easy to empathize with their suffering. But it is very hard for people to relate to violence when it's at the level

42.   Kogut, T. and Ritov, I. (2005), The "Identified Victim" effect: An identified group, or just a single individual?, *Journal of Behavioral Decision-Making*, 18, pp. 157-167.

of abstract statistics - anonymous casualties in countries where you have never been. You may understand the facts about massive abuses and huge numbers of people being killed, but you do not relate to it. Of course, the media plays an important role in building empathy towards certain victims, while presenting other victims as anonymous statistics.

JF   Yes, the media avoid personalizing certain atrocities.

RA   Your brain somehow cannot feel empathy towards numbers, it cannot scale to the dimensions of the tragedy. This also makes me think of the wars in Gaza and Syria, wars with thousands of casualties recorded by citizen journalists. The effect of learning about these tragedies is "desensitization"[43], something I am very familiar with because I experienced it growing up during a war and living my early adulthood in one of the most violent cities in the world. The most popular news outlet in Guatemala, the tabloid newspaper *Nuestro Diario*, features news of people being killed on its front page every single day. In such a way violence is normalized and routinized. When you see that there is no public outcry after heads are dumped in the Guatemalan National Congress,[44] or when 27 peasants are

43. To understand more about this concept, see Monroy-Hernandez et al, 'Narco' Emotions: Affect and Desensitization in Social Media during the Mexican Drug War, *Proceedings of CHI 2014*: https://archive.is/ZlCBN

44. See 'Heads dumped in Guatemala capital', *Reuters*: https://archive.is/x2pzW

decapitated,[45] including children, you realize that the place you are living in is experiencing a kind of collective illness of desensitization. And if even the local people don't care about such crimes, what can you expect from outsiders?

JF   Renata, I think you wanted to return to talking about the role of women?

RA   Yes, I think that women in the world of digital dissidence play key roles as leaders and dissenters, but that sometimes their work, contributions, and leadership are less visible as compared with men. In one way, ironically, it's kind of fortunate that their role is downplayed within their own community and dismissed by their governments, because that actually gives them greater room to act. Governments simply do not see women as key players therefore, that allows women to fly under the radar a little more.

JF   Why is that? Is it because of the idea of locking woman in jail is considered shameful? The majority of governments are run by men after all...

RA   Sadly, governments simply do not listen to women and media tend to ignore women in their reporting on them. The media are simply not reporting about the amazing

45.   See '27 killed in massacre in northern Guatemala; farm workers beheaded in lawless border region', *New York Daily News*: https://archive.is/GdsoL

things that dissident women are doing. For example, in my country, the fight against the mining industry[46] is led by women community leaders, and there are now attempts to charge them with sabotage and terrorism just for defending their territories. They are not live-tweeting and there is no hashtag for their cause, but they are right there fighting. The story is not covered in the media because reporting on women fighting against mining corporations conflicts with the corporate capture of media.

JF   But is this useful? Does it mean that they can effect more change?

RA   It depends. I can remember one of the first conversations that I had with Julian Assange when he said: "I do not respect anyone who has not been in prison." What he meant was that being in prison means that you have made so much trouble for the system that the only way for the system to deal with you is to lock you up and try to silence you. But with women, there are other ways to control and silence them.

---

46. See 'Guatemala women defenders defy Canadian mines and plead for help', *Rabble*: https://archive.is/3TWAm

SNOWDEN FORCED THEM TO TAKE OFF
THE MASK

AR   I wanted to return to the Snowden case. Glenn Green-
      wald, has justified his redactions and partial release of
      documents partly on the basis of wanting to keep peo-
      ple from harm, but he has also claimed that he and his
      colleagues are simply following Snowden's own wishes.
      Maybe this is a question that you can answer, since you
      spent quite a lot of time with Snowden. What is Snowden's
      stance?

SH   I wouldn't put words into Snowden's mouth. But you
      can look at all the public statements from the people
      involved in this and it's very confusing. One minute,
      it's claimed that Snowden gave all the documents to the
      journalists, and left it to them to make the decisions
      regarding releasing the material. The next minute Glenn
      is saying that Snowden is telling them what they can and
      can't publish. Then we hear that the government is telling
      them what to do based on supposed National Security
      concerns. Glenn and his colleagues change their argu-
      ments depending on who the audience is at any given
      time. Glenn said something very interesting when he was
      asked about WikiLeaks' decision to name the identity

of 'Country X'.[47, 48] To paraphrase from what I remember, he later said something like: "Yes, well, WikiLeaks, it turns out they were right in calling for that" and that there hadn't been any harm caused by releasing the name of the country. And then people actually thanked WikiLeaks for keeping the mainstream media, governments, and even Greenwald, honest. So I was joking with Julian that we should turn the WikiLeaks catchphrase of "Keeping the bastards honest" into "Keeping the bastards and *The Intercept* honest".

AR   Glenn's always referring to Snowden in his statements on Twitter. I wonder what Snowden thinks about that? Is it true that he thinks it's for the journalists to make the decisions regarding releasing documents? The journalists involved always seem to emphasize that Snowden doesn't support "dumping" the documents in their entirety.

JF   Yes, but WikiLeaks has never simply "dumped" material.

47. See Gawker, *Why Did Wikileaks Name "Country X" When Glenn Greenwald Wouldn't?*: https://archive.is/PJPNW
48. In a 2014 article published by The Intercept based on Snowden's revelations that showed the NSA collects data on all mobile phone calls from the Bahamas and another country, The Intercept redacted the name of the second country and only referred to it as Country X. They claimed they had "specific, credible concerns that" identifying the country "could lead to increased violence" there, though against whom and what was not explained. WikiLeaks stated that it did not agree with censoring a whole country who deserved to know this, especially when phone surveillance is used for drone strikes there, revealed that Country X was Afghanistan.

AR   I also sometimes wonder: how closely is Snowden actually following the whole release process?

RA   If you're a lawyer, you have an obligation to your client to respect what he or she wishes. If you're a journalist and you get a set of documents that are in the public interest, it really gets very ambiguous whether you should defer to the interests of the public or the wishes of your source. On the one hand, you are supposed to serve the public interest and provide the public with information that is accurate and complete, so that it can make better informed decisions. On the other hand, even if you know that you have in your possession important information documenting human rights violations or unprecedented abuses from corporations, your alleged source may insist on restricting the sharing of it.

SH   Is Snowden a "traitor" or a "hero"? People are split on this. My personal view is that Snowden is not a traitor at all. What he did was entirely in accordance with the US Constitution that he swore to uphold. The people that are committing unconstitutional acts, the ones that are really trampling on the Constitution, are those within the government and the US deep state. It really annoys me when people say that Snowden is a traitor. It's even more annoying when people say Assange is a traitor to the US, because he's not even American!

AR   What I find interesting, as a European, is that after the Iron Curtain came down the dominant narrative was that the

US were the goodies in the Cold War and that the US is the best friend of the Europeans. However when the Snowden revelations becaome public it became obvious that, in its use of mass surveillance, the US government doesn't respect the fundamental rights and freedoms of even allied countries. For instance, we learned that US security were tapping Angela Merkel's private mobile phone, and after this was reported in the media the US didn't even apologize. Obama's speech subsequent to the revelations was basically without content. It was just a non-statement. Nor did he apologize to other nations for violating their privacy. He did apologize to the American people and assured them that they are only being watched for their own good and in the name of national security. I find it very interesting how normal national and international surveillance has become. American citizens have become used to the idea that their government has the right to watch everybody else. Not just terrorists, but even citizens and elected officials of allied nations: Basically, everybody! What Edward Snowden did was force them to take off the mask and admit these things.

RA   As neither a European nor an American citizen, I have a very different perspective. For me, the NSA revelations were not shocking at all, because in my country all our rights have been eroded by the DEA as part of the War on Drugs. And even before that, all our rights of free speech and political expression were trampled in the course of the Cold War - dissidents were all labelled as socialists or communists. And Latin America was, until very recently, treated as "America's backyard". We are geographically and culturally very close to the US. We grow up with American culture and someone who is Latin American has a place within American culture, but as 'the Other'. We grow up with this sense that we are second-class citizens of the world. But what is interesting to me regarding this question of whether Snowden is a "hero" or a "traitor" is the difference between the way Edward Snowden and Chelsea Manning are viewed. Unlike Chelsea Manning, many perceive Edward Snowden as an exemplary citizen who did his duty. His actions are seen as incredibly courageous because he thought about them in terms of his commitment to the US constitution. For me, the real "constitution" is the universally recognized human rights principles enshrined in the Universal Declaration of Human Rights. That's my "constitution." I'm a global citizen, I don't care about the Guatemalan Constitution, which was approved during the war period.

SH   My country doesn't even have a constitution!

RA   The debate around the NSA revelations is generally very centered on the US. It's a debate that's focused on the question of constitutionality. If you compare the NSA revelations with those of Chelsea Manning, it's radically different. It's like comparing apples with oranges. In contrast to the desensitization we talked about earlier, Chelsea showed an unprecedented level of empathy and commitment to human rights. A young American person, who had never travelled to the Middle East before, was showing concern for the victims of American power - for the children in the *Collateral Murder* video,[49] and was moved to political action by seeing the murdering and maiming of children and journalists. Chelsea Manning decided to sacrifice both her life and future in the fight for international justice, beyond US borders. That future maybe wasn't especially bright, but at least she had a job. Chelsea Manning is my hero. I really deeply admire her and her commitment to human rights and internationalism. By contrast the NSA revelations have resulted in a much more localized struggle, primarily in the United States.

SH   Within the US, it's not so uncommon for people to see Snowden as a hero. But the reason they celebrate and support Snowden so much is due to the fact that he revealed that the US government was spying on the US public. It's all very US-centric.

AR   Yes, it's easier for people in the West to take his side because he can be perceived as a patriot who was acting in accord with the US constitution. For me, personally, I find patriotism suspicious and I despise nationalism.

49.   See CollateralMurder.com: http://www.collateralmurder.com/en/img/imgi-raq/Sayad-and-Doaha.jpg.html

SH   Just one little side point: As heroic as Snowden was in what he actually did, there was something that really annoyed me about the public's reaction – particularly in the US, but also elsewhere. Much of the public seemed to believe that Snowden's actions were more effective than Manning's. Actually, if you look at it objectively, what Snowden did was heroic but so far, to date, the actual effects have largely been limited to fostering a debate and greater consciousness of surveillance. By contrast, Manning is widely credited with having helped to expedite US withdrawal from Iraq and with having contributed to the Arab Spring – very significant international events.

The only concrete effects of the NSA revelations so far are that, firstly, Brazil is going to invest in its own internet infrastructure. Which is great news, but is probably something that was going to happen anyway. And, secondly, US security agencies were shown to be illegally holding phone data indefinitely, which resulted in a law change that allows them to legally continue to harvest and keep phone data. That's not to say there won't be more significant consequences of the NSA revelations at some point, but right now Chelsea Manning has had more impact than Snowden. The public response, according to which Snowden supposedly effected major changes whilst Manning didn't, really upsets me. It upsets me because, firstly, it's just factually incorrect – Manning helped stop a war and start a revolution! And, secondly, it annoys me because I don't think we should be creating this sort of 'competition' of effectiveness in the first place. I don't think comparisons of effectiveness are helpful. The actions of both

Snowden and Manning are hugely heroic. But it feels like the public have made this supposed competition between the two a large part of the story.

AR   I disagree, I think It's the press that has caused this.

RA   I agree, it's the media.

AR   Most people I encounter don't talk in terms of these competitive comparisons. I did a lot of panels and discussions on both Manning and the NSA revelations when I wrote and staged my play about WikiLeaks.[50] It was never a big issue. When I do the panels, I'm always positively surprised by the audience. They're not as stupid as they're constantly portrayed as being. Nobody I spoke to ever denigrated Manning's actions.

SH   Maybe I'm wrong. Maybe it's the press that's made it competitive. But, for example, at the Chaos Computer Club congress (CCC)[51] Snowden posters were everywhere with the slogan "Asylum for Snowden!" Snowden has asylum already, whereas Manning is now stuck for 35 years in prison.[52] I saw barely any Manning posters at CCC, but there were Snowden posters and stickers everywhere. He's

---

50. *Assassinate Assange*, which was staged in Berlin, Hamburg, Cologne and Vienna in 2012. See: https://archive.is/wWdC3

51. The 30th Chaos Communication Congress (30C3) in Hamburg, 27–30 December 2013, see: https://archive.is/90dou

52. At time of publication Chelsea Manning has been released from prison after President Barack Obama commuted her sentence before his presidency ended.

become part of the collective psyche in a way that Manning hasn't. People seem to be more supportive of Snowden and seem to perceive this difference between his actions and Chelsea's actions. And a lot of it - and I think you're right that it is the press – is actually because of the way in which the NSA documents have been published. Journalists like Greenwald have made this big thing out of how responsibly and carefully they are publishing the documents. I think that's actually what's pitted these two whistleblowers, particularly within the arena of US media, against each other. The US media has settled on one of them as being and more correct and virtuous than the other. And I think it is wrong. They both committed heroic acts. They should both be supported equally.

RA   For me, the most interesting thing about WikiLeaks is that it is helping to make information part of the commons again. I think people perceive this better in Latin America. In Latin America, it's not about Assange, it's not about Manning, it's not about Snowden – it's about the content. The explosive thing is the revelations, not the whistleblowers themselves. And the amazing thing is that, for the first time, people who can't speak English (because we still have this horrible language barrier and very little resources for translation) could actually read these documents in their entirety. That is really ground-breaking. It's a first for Latin American journalism.

COMPLETELY ISOLATED IN A NON-PLACE PLACE

AR   Finally, going back to Snowden again. Can you tell us a little bit about your whole experience, or adventure, with him? Because I think it's difficult to imagine what happened to you. You went to Hong Kong to help Snowden and you ended up spending months with him in a Moscow airport. I would like to hear about that first-hand.

SH   If we put aside the time spent in Hong Kong for a moment, there was a very interesting aspect to this experience that I only understood once I was in Berlin. People subsequently said to me: "It must have been so exciting! They forced Evo Morales' plane to land, and so many other extraordinary things happened!" And, indeed I was a part of all this, these huge worldwide events that were being followed by so many people. But the strange thing is that, even when you're at the center of these events you don't feel any of this excitement. We were simply stuck in in a transit zone of an airport. And, of course, we didn't have anything to do with Morales' plane being grounded.[53]

53.   During a flight home from Moscow, the Bolivian presidential plane carrying President Evo Morales was forced to re-route and land in Vienna over false rumours that Edward Snowden was on board. See 'Political Interference': https://www.freesnowden.is/political-interference/#forced-landing

AR   But did you hear about it?

SH   Yes, we were following the news, which is what made it such a bizarre, surreal experience. This situation where you are central to what's happening, but without having any connection to it in a concrete, physical way. Actually, people who saw Morales' plane being grounded and talked with their friends about it in the pub that evening going, "My god! My god! Did you see?" – even those people would have had more of a connection with reality, because they were living in the world in which such things were going on. Whereas we were stuck in this weird isolated transit zone. It was a place that's a non-place, a place outside of the world of nationalities and countries. We were non-participants in these incredible events that were happening outside of the zone.

AR   Could you describe what it was like in the transit zone? What does it mean to be in a non-place? Where did you live and sleep?

SH   The transit zone had a hotel, but I can't really go into more specific details. Lots of people were just passing through this place. There's this weird dynamic whereby you're in Russia but you're not really in Russia. Everybody else is just passing through the zone, and you're just stuck there.

AR   Did you have any way to communicate with the outside world?

SH   We were able to access the internet while we were there.

AR   And you were completely isolated from other human beings?

SH   Completely isolated in this non-place place. And, like I said, all this stuff was going on around us, these massive worldwide events that people were talking about. We could see it all happening but only on the internet. Clearly everyone was talking about it with their friends and governments around the world were obviously discussing it. And I was, in a way, central to it yet completely and utterly disconnected from it at the same time.

AR   Your experience of the transit zone reminds me of Sartre's play, *No Exit,* in which three people are locked forever in just one room. In the play, the room is a version of purgatory.

RA   It was very interesting to see you locked in one place with Snowden, while Julian was trapped in the Ecuadorian embassy at the same time. And because of modern technology there was this interaction between these two isolated places. It was impressive to see that with the right tools, people can continue to have a powerful effect even under such conditions in what are, perhaps, the two most surveilled countries in the world – the UK and Russia. Seeing the possibilities for continuing to effect change under such conditions has quite a powerful demonstration effect in my opinion. For me, it was also an exciting experience to see the other side: to see what was going on in the Ecuadorian embassy while you were in the air. In the embassy we were so worried about surveillance that we didn't even want to check the flight path of the plane, or even open a browser in case we were being observed. It was also a very surreal situation, because Julian's birthday party was happening at the same time.

SH   No one knew what was going on. I was trying to send over basic information like the flight details, so that someone had them and knew what was happening. And Julian was running in and out of his party... It was total chaos. I was about to get on a flight with an alleged "fugitive", and no one was able to talk to me! Returning, though, to Renata's point about being locked in a room - that period gave me a small but very real insight into Julian's situation. I discovered that however much you sympathize, however hard you might try to understand it, you have absolutely no idea what it's like to be confined in a small space like that. I got a glimpse of it during my experience. For example, when we finally left the transit zone my eyes physically hurt due to lack of sunlight and visual-field depth during my confinement. And, of course, I was in that situation for just one month - not years. I now realize how little I can understand how emotionally and physically traumatic the situation must be for him. I don't know how he does it. He must have great strength and tenacity.

RA   It was an absolutely crazy situation because, instead of enjoying his birthday party, he was overseeing all of the WikiLeaks team, who were working on trying to save

Snowden, but at the same time he was trying to deal with the guests at the party. And he had to stay alert to the computer and time zone differences and beating the surveillance of the UK government, and observing all these super-high security protocols. The next day we had a visit from Pussy Riot! Not the ones who were in prison, obviously, but the ones who remained anonymous. We were in the living room of the embassy, hanging out with people from Pussy Riot who oppose the Russian regime, while you were still in the air heading to Russia.

AR   So basically, you came to Russia and it became clear you could not continue on the one flight. Because I remember they posted these pictures of the empty seat. This is where Snowden was supposed to sit. There was a sort of poetry in it, right?

RA   It was Ironic. Poor journalists, who are usually underpaid and overworked, finally managed to take a vacation in Cuba.[54]

SH   We had flights booked all the way to Latin America.

AR   But Snowden's passport was cancelled.

SH   Generally, the US standard procedure when they issue an extradition warrant is that they cancel your passport. We

---

54. The Washington Post. Caitlin Dewey. Reporters who chased Snowden to Havana now enjoying unexpected tropical vacations: https://archive. is/3uPeM

had obviously done a lot of work to ensure that we could get out of Hong Kong, which was imperative because of the asylum and extradition laws in Hong Kong. If we hadn't got him out of Hong Kong he would be in prison right now, either there or in the US. So getting out of Hong Kong was imperative. And because of the work we did, we were able to ensure he could exit legally. But then the US definitively cancelled his passport, after we had left Hong Kong. So then, of course, we got to Moscow and we needed to check-in for the next flight. It had to be a separate check-in because of the time difference between the two flights. You couldn't have done it from within Hong Kong, so we actually had to check-in again. But by then his passport had been cancelled. The US government trapped him there.

AR   We talked before about the differences between Manning and Snowden. You spent a lot of time with Snowden. Did you have discussions about how the material should be released? And about this question of patriotism? Or did you avoid these topics?

SH   He's very much of the opinion that he's given this information to journalists, and that it's up to them to choose what to do with that information. He believes it's the responsibility of the journalists to decide what's in the public interest.

AR   But how did he decide who to give the documents to? What was his criteria for that?

SH   That definitely would be a question to ask him. He's said publicly that it's US information and therefore it's for US journalists to decide what is in the US public interest.

AR   Did you question him regarding his patriotism?

SH   He is hugely patriotic. We would have jokes about it, because I'm just not a patriotic person at all, and I generally find patriotic Americans annoying. So, we would have many jokey discussions about this. Even if I disagree with being patriotic – because I see things in a more global sense – it does really annoy me when people say that he is a traitor, because he clearly isn't. Legally speaking, he did the right thing. Ethically, he did the right thing. And saying that he is a traitor, when he's actually one of the most loyal, patriotic people I've met, is completely, incorrect. And it really upsets me.

RA   It's fascinating, because he's really a gentleman; he's really well-educated, really mild-mannered.

SH   He's not a high school dropout, as the US government likes to portray him.

AR   Does he have a university degree?

RA   He doesn't, but he's well-read, and in general, he's a very kind, gentle, and likeable person. He grew up using technology in a middle-class American family and is somewhat apolitical, in the way all the tech community is.

AR   It's astounding to me that he's apolitical.

RA   Perhaps that's not the best way of putting it, but he certainly would not define himself as being on the Right or the Left.

SH   He's not attached himself to any specific party or ideology.

RA   Exactly. For me it was quite shocking that someone the same age as myself was doing this. Because, with the exception of Manning, most of the news we get is always about people in their fifties, or even older. And this guy, a young man, at a very mid-level position in terms of government, made these extraordinary things happen. It shows that the deep surveillance state, has grown so big that it has lost control of what it collects and even of its own personnel to some extent. Its architecture of "Collect It All"[55] makes fulfilling its own mission really difficult, because of the sheer volume of material they have to sift through.

SH   I think there's a problem with any organization that becomes too large. Whether it's the state, a media organization, or a corporation - they acquire a certain institutional character. Certain rules evolve, and a certain

55. See 'Collect It All is an explicit Five Eyes goal' in Revelations section, Free Snowden:https://www.freesnowden.is/revelations/#collect-it-all-is-an-explicit-five-eyes-goal

organizational culture, and they become too large. They become unruly and, in fact, pretty uncontrollable, even as they try to assert control over others. If you look, for example, at the NSA – well, that's how Petraeus[56] got caught when he showed classified material to someone he was having an affair with. The institutional culture of the NSA encouraged him to believe he could get away with it. I acquired a better understanding of the way institutional cultures can affect people when we worked with the New York Times on the Iraq War Logs. The journalists at the Times wouldn't use the word "torture", not because they were banned from doing so, but because they were so used to working intimately with the government that it wouldn't even occur to them to use the term. It had become part of their institutional and organizational culture that they operated closely with the government. That meant that they tended to act in a certain way. I had a very interesting conversation with a guy from the New York Times when we were working on CableGate. We went out for a dinner and one of their head journalists was telling me about how he'd started off in the *New York Times* as an intern and stayed with them through his whole career.

56. The Petraeus scandal was a series of events that garnered strong media attention when an extramarital affair between retired four-star general David Petraeus, then Director of the Central Intelligence Agency (CIA), and his biographer Paula Broadwell, to whom he had given unauthorised access to top-secret information, became public. It eventually led to his prosecution. See timeline: https://archive.is/W9eH1

He was very proud of having spent his entire career at the *Times*. I asked him whether he felt he had become institutionalized at all, and actually, to his credit, after thinking about it for a bit, he admitted that he probably had. So, even by their own admission, these people's brains become warped by the organizational culture. And there's really no hope for us if these huge international organizations are controlling everything, even making everybody who works for them think in a certain way. That's actually one of the most interesting things about Snowden and Manning specifically: they did manage to break out of the culture of the organizations they were embedded in. Jeremy Hammond came from a very different background and was never within one of these institutions, but Snowden and Manning are examples of people that had grown up with the internet. So, even when they then joined these institutions, their primary allegiance was to the freedoms and ideals they associate with the internet. The internet can potentially be a revolutionary force at this historical moment. It's global, it brings a sense of freedom and empowerment to its users, and gives the public greater access to information. And when these freedoms are taken away, people like Snowden and Manning feel this quite keenly because they're so used to sharing information. They've grown up with the idea that free flow of information is normal. I think that's why Manning and Snowden were able to break out of the ideology of the institutions they were working for.

JF   What is needed to have a true revolutionary moment? What is needed to truly make the internet a revolutionary force?

SH   I think there is certainly a key element to revolutions that we can see throughout history and that is 'the Square'. In any revolution we see people congregating in public squares to exchange ideas and formulate plans. The internet provides a modern global equivalent to the square while still potentially aiding community-building at a more local level. Of course, right now the internet is being increasingly censored and removed from public control and oversight, through proprietary software and so on. The curtailment of internet freedom inhibits people's ability to organize and exchange ideas, and also gives rise to a chilling effect. Despite the potential revolutionary possibilities inherent in the internet, people don't use it for such purposes because they fear surveillance, even if they are not actually being monitored. And this problem is compounded in the West, because we are gathering less and less in public spaces. So we have lost the custom of regularly meeting in a really free space for the exchange of ideas – whether online or offline - which is a precondition for any revolution.

However, in the short term the decline in internet freedom might have some beneficial consequences. Sometimes, when things have moved so far in the wrong direction people become sufficiently motivated to push back against the powerful. In the wake of the

WikiLeaks and Snowden revelations I think people perceive that the state of online privacy and freedoms is actually getting worse. As people have come increasingly to understand how dire the prospects for online privacy and freedoms are most of the offending governments have doubled down on their efforts to surveil us and further reduce our ability to protect ourselves. Governments have sought to normalize what was once clandestine, and to place what used to be illegal surveillance on a legal footing.

And this also ties into the discourse of the War on Terror. For example, in the UK the then Prime Minister, David Cameron, wanted to ban end-to-end encryption.[57] This drift towards increasing repression seems to have actually been strengthened, not weakened, by the Snowden revelations. The trajectories of public opinion and government policy on these issues are seemingly in opposite directions. In some ways I actually hope the situation gets much worse. Maybe then the public will get to the stage where everyone is ready to fight back hard and things can change. But that needs to happen quickly, before the balance of power is skewed so far in favor of governments that there is no hope of ever restoring a degree of equilibrium.

AR   Personally I'm not sure if the internet was ever a revolutionary force. It certainly represents a technological revolution. But it is a tool that can be used for many things, both good as well as bad. At the moment we are faced with

57.   For more details about the UK encryption ban, see 'No U-turn: David Cameron still wants to break encryption', *Wired*: https://archive.is/ Mynkm

the internet being used as a mass surveillance tool by governments, so the only way to win back a degree of control is through encryption. It is the only tool for self-defense at the moment.

RA   In my opinion we need to get rid of borders, we need to get rid of passports, copyright, and patents. We need to get rid of the rigid structures of the past that are limiting exchange and collective creation in the present. The only solution to overcome the transnational totalitarianism that we are witnessing, and that Angela described so well, is to design new architectures of revolution. We need to imagine new institutions that could enhance the power of decentralized political action.

We don't necessarily need to overthrow the current system to beat it. We could either hack it or repurpose it for our own need, or simply abandon it in favor of our own system. What I'm thinking of are things like WikiLeaks' hacking journalism, libraries and archives to make them freely available. I'm thinking of blockchain[58] and Bitcoin as valid, robust, and decentralized alternatives to the collapsing monetary system. Or again, I'm thinking of open-sourced, peer-to-peer institutions that operate across borders. Of course, P2P exchanges are as old as humanity, but the scale and speed of non-commercial P2P exchange is better than it has ever

58.   See 'Why Blockchains Could Transform How the Economy Works', *Wall Street Journal*: https://archive.is/qVrG3

been because of advances in communications infrastructure and technology.

In fact, the battle for control of infrastructure is another front we need to fight on if we want to see the next revolution happen. Without exercising some degree of control over the infrastructure of the internet, we will always have very limited time in which to act before our operations are disrupted or shut down. It's not good enough to operate in this kind of 'hit and run' manner that we are forced to adopt because we don't have any control over the infrastructure. Always occupying the position of mere resistance is too precarious and not sustainable. And it is certainly not appealing to broader populations when all we can offer is constantly resisting, fighting, and suffering. We need to make our struggle more and more joyful in order to bring more people over to our side. If we have created the largest totalitarian tool that has ever existed, maybe it is time to destroy it. And the act of getting rid of it, as it was with the biblical Tower of Babel, will be revolutionary in itself. Or, as I said previously, we need to invent and create a real alternative that builds the foundations of our future, into its design. And we certainly need to build a new common, global communications infrastructure that follows different design principles to the Internet as it is currently constituted.

JF   Is it a problem of the traditional left that it doesn't understand the power – or for that matter the dangers – inherent in technology?

RA   The left often excludes the new and the different from their exclusive club. They turn a blind eye to the wrongs of those on their side, and take an inconsistent approach to universal human rights. The left's silence on the Aleppo massacre is a good example of this. Perhaps the left's institutional culture is too male, too white. Its adherents always looks to the past for its organizational forms rather than reinventing itself anew. Self-proclaimed old-school leftists actually adopt much of the Same formalities and exclusivity that exists on the Right, but in a more precarious position. They've also adopted a very rigid one-size-fits-all solution for a very unequal world, at a time when regions of the global south are just starting to explore and experiment in new and unique ways. A famous writer from my country Guatemala, Tito Monterroso, wrote a poem intended to illustrate the Right: "When he awoke, the dinosaur was still there." Sadly, the left became that dinosaur. One thinks of the kind of leftist you see wearing a faded Che Guevara t-shirt, quoting Trotsky, sipping wine and ranting about the Right while ignoring his own privilege as a well-travelled, educated man. Leftist candidates in my country always come from such backgrounds: educated at La Sorbonne, angry, extremely Westernized, boring and patronizing. They are still dreaming about a revolution that happened more than 70 years ago; dreaming about a political moment that will never repeat because the world has changed too much. The problem of the left is their loyalty to their old dreams, their old institutions, which once worked, but no longer do.

The most exciting movements of the last five years grew among young people, connected online but taking their struggles to the square. We need to start from there, from rejection of the current system to imagining the next one. But we are running out of time and, if we are not careful, not even resistance will be possible anymore. We need to start developing a strategy now.

AR   I largely agree with Renata's description of the left. I can only add that the typical Eurocentric, left, white male-type is not only ignoring technology, but is even ignoring the danger that comes from the neoliberal ideology emanating from Silicon Valley. I would even go so far as to say that there are two aggressively expanding global movements at the moment: one is the brutal Islamist ideology of Daesh (ISIS) in the East, and diametrically opposed to that, Silicon Valley capitalism in the West. They are both movements that seem to attract young people, obviously for different reasons. Whether we like it or not, they are the most compelling youth movements of our time.

Daesh appears to be more obviously sinister - it's a death cult masquerading as a religious movement. However, the sunny, cheerful surface of the tech start-ups in California cannot really hide the cold, neoliberal ideology of the people who run these companies. The traditional left is still preoccupied with the traditional finance capitalism of Wall Street, which they feel able to categorize and analyze. But while they are contemplating finance they are failing to see that, the ideology of Silicon Valley is in danger of conquering the world. It is about time to address that, to properly analyze Silicon Valley and its attendant ideology, and take action against it.

SH   I am not sure if it's a problem for the 'traditional Left' per se, but more of a generational and demographic problem. Advances in technology are happening so quickly that it's difficult for anyone that hasn't grown up with these technologies to have any chance of keeping up. It is harder for older people to build up any real understanding of the possibilities and issues surrounding technology. Certainly, for society as a whole, understanding the power and danger of technology is vital if it is to be used to our advantage. Since technology is being used to censor and surveil us, we can't protect ourselves or fight on this terrain without understanding the technology ourselves. But, like an AK47, technology has the potential to be a balancing force. Take encryption: one lone citizen can encrypt something and, if done right, the NSA can't access the information. As in past conflicts, once guerrillas had access to firearms, the balance of power was shifted in favor of ordinary people. It may be that the computer is the AK47 of our age. It can be used by powerful interests to attack us, but it's also possible for citizens to arm ourselves with the same technology and fight back.

To me, the biggest issue we face is the lack of public awareness around government propaganda. It's all around us and yet most people don't see it for what it is. It's what allows governments to increasingly surveil, under the guise of "national security." Even though governments have been unable to produce any evidence that mass surveillance has thwarted terror attacks, propaganda has successfully established among the public the idea that the threat of terrorism justifies surveillance. Propaganda is what allows governments to unfairly prosecute publishers and whistleblowers with propaganda campaigns that villainize them and make people fear associating with such individuals and organizations. Propaganda prevents people from understanding what WikiLeaks does and why it is so important. We've already touched on it a number of times in this conversation: did WikiLeaks harm or help? Is Snowden a hero or a traitor? Does surveillance protect or harm us? Is Manning a political prisoner or a criminal? The answers to all these questions relate to the difference between fact and truth. There are many facts around all of these questions, but the truth is something larger, which rises out of the confluence of those facts. The current truth of our time is being fought over in the minds of people, a propaganda war, between what governments say they do and what our work shows they do.

CODA

At the conclusion of their exchange, Avila, Harrison and Richter agreed to meet again within the next year to discuss how the politics of the internet was developing, and whether their perspectives had changed. When, in July 2016, that meeting eventually took place, it was clear that a series of very pronounced changes were taking place in Western society. The prolongation and escalation of the war in Syria as a regional confrontation between NATO and Russia had given rise to tensions in Eastern Europe, and the terrorist franchise of Daesh, the so-called "Islamic State," had launched lethal terrorist attacks in European capitals. On January 7, 2015, two gunmen killed twelve staff members of the Parisian satirical magazine, *Charlie Hebdo*,[59] along with other members of the public. On November 13, a series of lethal attacks were again carried out in Paris killing a total of 130 people, including the massacre of 89 people at the Bataclan Theater. By the end of the 2015, the French government had introduced emergency legislation granting unprecedented police powers and suspended many civil liberties for an indefinite period. Framing the attacks as the

---

59. A French weekly satirical magazine which was attacked by terrorist gunmen in January 2015, killing 12 people. See Charlie Hebdo attack: three days of terror, BBC https://archive.is/9AP4r

consequence of the lack of military intervention in Syria, both the UK and French governments authorized direct military involvement in that country.

A further series of terrorist attacks took place during the Spring and Summer of 2016. On March 22, three coordinated suicide bombings in Brussels killed 32 people and injured over 300. On July 14, during the celebrations for Bastille Day, a cargo truck was used as a weapon on the Promenade des Anglais in Nice, killing 86 people and injuring 434. And on July 22, an 18-year-old gunman shot dead ten people and injured 36 at a shopping mall in Munich. Despite widely different profiles and motives, the killers were portrayed by the mainstream Western press as part of a new monolithic terrorist threat, and seized upon by Western governments eager to enhance their police and intelligence surveillance powers. Repressive surveillance laws, such as the UK's IP Bill, gathered steam. A spate of press comments from senior intelligence officials, both on and off the record, sought to argue that Edward Snowden's disclosures were the main reason the terrorist plots had not been foiled before they happened, despite the fact that none of the terrorists were found to have used encryption, and most were already known to the authorities. In Turkey, a failed coup d'état on July 15, 2016 led to increased repression under the Erdogan government, resulting in the mass imprisonment of academics, journalists, civil society workers, and the implementation of even more extreme internet surveillance and censorship measures than those that had existed prior to the failed coup.

Contemplating these developments, Avila, Harrison, and Richter felt it was necessary to revisit the cautious optimism of their earlier discussion, and to discuss the implications of these events for the movement for online freedom of information, transparency, accountability, journalism and the protection of privacy.

SH   I think the documents he disclosed certainly showed how surveillance is involved in breaches of our privacy. They did not necessarily show that surveillance harms our security themselves, though I would argue it does. However, the documents did revealed that mass surveillance is not actually helping to foil terrorist attacks. Consider in the case of the Charlie Hebdo attacks and the later Paris attacks. The perpetrators were already known to the French government as persons of interest, and they used conventional methods of communication. I think two things become apparent when we consider such attacks in the context of the NSA revelations. Firstly, in spite of immense global mass surveillance on the part of Western governments, terrorist attacks continue, and secondly that Snowden's disclosures have not undermined the ability of intelligence agencies to "catch the terrorists." Even so, the response of the French state to these attacks has been to declare an indefinite state of emergency and to increase their own powers of surveillance. And yet the attacks keep on happening.

I think the problem we now face is that too many people accept state propaganda, that tells them that "national security" justifies this unprecedented levels of surveillance. The French surveillance measures are particularly egregious, especially given the fact that the emergency regime under which they are sanctioned continues indefinitely. For example, just after introducing the state of emergency, the authorities began to use it primarily against climate change activists. It's upsetting to me that more people don't understand that "national security" is routinely used to justify enhanced police powers, that are not designed to protect us.

THE WEST ONLY REACTS WITH OUTRAGE
WHEN VICTIMS ARE WHITE

JF   Do you think the surveillance state has become stronger
          since Edward Snowden's revelations? And if so, how do
          you explain that - given that Snowden revealed that sur-
          veillance was endangering our private lives and security?

AR   I agree, I think that terrorist attacks of this kind cannot be
          stopped with the usual tools. Not only is mass surveillance
          not rational in my opinion, but it's also not effective. When
          I interviewed Bill Binney[60] that's exactly what he said.
          And when you consider the attacks in Munich and Würz-
          burg - these were perpetrated by teenagers, one of them
          a 16-year-old girl. They were not hardened terrorists, but
          troubled teenagers in a difficult phase of their lives. They
          weren't operating according to a master plan from ISIS.
          ISIS just sow the ideological seeds in the heads of these
          people and they didn't require any strategy or real planning
          to do what they did, and so surveillance was never going to
          stop them. They simply took a gun and started shooting.
          This is a situation where if people are determined to carry

60.   William Binney is a former high-ranking NSA official who turned whis-
      tleblower over the expansion of its surveillance programme after 9/11.
      See Angela Richter, Supernerds: Conversations with Heroes, 2015.

out an attack it's almost impossible to stop them. Furthermore, often these "foreign" terrorists are not foreign at all. For instance, this "Iranian" guy in Munich was a German actually and he even shouted that he was a German while threatening to kill people. I mean, the ideology propagated by groups like ISIS is more like a contagion and I don't think that surveillance can prevent attacks like this.

SH Yeah, it's an interesting point regarding the nationalities of people carrying out these attacks. In the case of the Paris attacks they were predominantly European-born but had become radicalized because of their experience of racism. It emerged from leaked documents last year that the Pentagon actually knew that the foreign policy decisions made by the US and French governments, intervention in Libya for example, were going to exacerbate the radicalization of Muslims all around the world. And yet they continued – people like Hillary Clinton at the State Department continued – despite strong advice to the contrary from the Pentagon.

RA The interesting thing is that, from my perspective, the only community that quickly reacted to the Snowden revelations in their own interests was the surveillance community. Fast-tracked legal reforms took place all over the world to basically legalize what their intelligence agencies were already doing in partnership with the US. And they did it very quickly, very efficiently, with the complete support of legislative bodies that passed laws so they could legalize what had been criminal activity. It was kind of absurd to see the outrage. "Oh my God, now the intelligence services want to do this or that in different countries," when the only thing that they were doing was covering their tracks and covering their backs, in countries like France, the Netherlands and UK. In others, the changes were pushed via cybercrime laws.

Their skill in reacting to the revelations has resulted in the validation and normalization of a system of global surveillance. Their strategy was quite remarkable. They used this combination of the rhetoric of fear and the European security crisis, to pass these laws as soon as possible, so they would not be legally liable. Surveillance capitalism, combined with the rise of the racist Right is what we now have to live with. Why did they pass these laws? Because they knew that they were hacking private systems, they knew that they were violating all sorts of human rights, and if they didn't pass those laws as soon as possible they would be criminally liable. Another important aspect of the recent terror attacks in Europe is the media focus on attacks that target people with a specific Western, middle-class lifestyle. We only notice terrorism when It happens in Europe, even though these kind of attacks are happening on a much larger scale everywhere. But it seems like the West only reacts with outrage when the victims are white.

SH   Yes.

RA   From the reactions to the latest wave of attacks in Europe, it is evident not only that racism is increasing, but that it is

also becoming normalized and acceptable. We are returning to a situation where people feel able to express racism
openly. I think that in the past people would cloak their
racism because of the memory of the atrocities of the Nazi
regime was too close. But now people feel free again to
express unvarnished racism.

SH   Yes. It returns us to the question of dissent, which we were
talking about during our last conversation.

RA   Yes, and what is more worrying is that, after the horrors of
WWII, progressively we had built mechanisms to prevent
violence and racism, but in the last decade or two those
mechanisms are simply falling apart. Especially if you consider the way democracy is working now in Europe, and
how pre-established human rights safeguards and systems
are defunded, dismantled, or circumvented. That's the
trend I'm seeing everywhere, not only in Europe. A per-
sistent state of emergency, exceptional laws, exceptional
powers, but also military interventions that are more open
and more cynical than before.

WE DON'T HAVE GOVERNMENT, WE HAVE GOOGLEMENT

JF   But what about the private sector? What role is Silicon Valley playing in all of this?

RA   The intervention of Silicon Valley, not only in Washington politics, but in global politics is now open, and seemingly unstoppable. Its scope has moved far beyond just facilitating communications. Silicon Valley is pushing really hard to take on functions that used to be performed by national governments, but globally and at a cost that local providers cannot compete with. Often the cost to replace the communications infrastructure of an entire institution is very marginal, but the price ordinary citizens pay is our data. The political influence and importance of Silicon Valley is really growing and the leaders of the major tech corporations are often received by governments with the honors that correspond to a head of state. One example of this is how these guys from Microsoft or Google are received by the heads of states of countries like India and Cuba as their

61. The Register: "Google chair Eric Schmidt reportedly visits Cuba" 2014 https://archive.is/3y1WD
The Guardian: "Eric Schmidt in North Korea: Google chairman's step into the unknown" 2013 https://archive.is/LekB8
The Wall Street Journal: Google's Schmidt Visits India 2013 https://archive.is/jvGbo

equals.[61] Never before in our time was the owner of a company received with such deference.

RA   It happens the other way around as well, because now you see politicians stopping by Washington and then they fly to Silicon Valley – that didn't happen before. I mean, politicians would visit factories of course, but now they go on official visits to Silicon Valley.[62] The wealth that these companies have is larger than many countries put together! It's a new form of global oligarchy that is impacting everything.

What I want to also make clear is that when we had our first conversation we were still a little bit hopeful on the questions of change and whether technology will actually empower. And now I'm just less and less hopeful.

It is clear, for instance, that the technology is creating a dangerous divide in wider society. Jobs in the most unstable and fragile countries and the precarious sectors of all societies are going to disappear soon. There is no way to catch up and fix the imbalances in time. So, while they will be able to connect to the internet, the marginalized won't be able to use it for effecting meaningful change in their lives. They will simply be connected to devices that control, measure, monitor, and predict. And the dangerous levels of inequality in the world today will obviously bring more instability and war.

62. Bloomberg: "Obama's Visit to Silicon Valley Is a Big Win for Apple Pay" 2015 https://archive.is/
     Indian Express: "PM Modi to Silicon Valley: Digital India 'unmatched in history'" 2015 https://archive.is/Zcm92

SH   There were private companies that were contracted by the CIA before – I mean, Snowden came from one – but the role of private tech companies has rapidly increased. They're not even contracted by the state necessarily anymore, they're just a revolving door between these corporations and governments. It has become one big amorphous blob. The term "Googlement" came up two years ago...

AR   Ah yes, Googlement. We don't have government, we have Googlement.

JF   Who was the genius who coined that?

SH   I think you [points at RA] were talking about it. And you [points at AR] said the word. I think that is really what we can see now except it's not just that Google is being *used* by the government or is *collaborating* with the government. Google has actually been integrated with the government in a really frightening way.

AR   Yes. It's totally in the open, that's right. During our last conversation I compared the Silicon Valley ideology (with its start-ups, its hysteria, its gadgets, all the apps, all the lifestyle that goes with it, and this fantasy of a light Western easy lifestyle) and I compared it to the other side – the opposed ideology of the death cult of ISIS. But now I wouldn't even compare the two because I think that the Silicon Valley ideology is way more dangerous than ISIS, because, at a global level, it's so much more powerful.

FROM ARTIFICIAL INTELLIGENCE
TO SUPER-INTELLIGENCE

RA   ISIS wants to occupy territory and to have control over resources and to create a state. Their final aim is very concrete and tangible. In the case of Silicon Valley, their domination is in our minds and that's a far more dangerous thing. I mean, we have experimented with artificial intelligence, but we have yet to experiment with super-intelligence, and these guys in Silicon Valley will have in their hands the power to control a machine that's more intelligent than humans. The people who will control this machine have a very specific ideology and set of ethics and the machine will continuously be getting more sophisticated due to all the input that we give to it. It will be a machine that can predict governments, that can predict the behavior of humanity. And so, that's a huge problem. Who will govern that machine, and *how* are we going to do it?

And then there's the DeepMind project. I met the guy behind Deep-Mind at a dinner party at Google HQ in London. The dinner was very interesting because we had the inventor of the web sitting on one side, parliamentarians from the UK government on the other side, some celebrities and musicians, and then the rest of the table was Google executives. The DeepMind guy gave the keynote speech.

He was bragging about how his machine was so efficient in eliminating targets and how precise and efficient it was at eliminating targets faster than a human mind, basically, and how good combat robots would be for the world because they would reduce the number of civilian casualties. A musician was there, listening, horrified, and he said, "Yes, but this is still a killing machine, right?"

AR   Yes, that's really scary. Also, I just read today that Google have stopped using their old motto: "Don't Be Evil".

SH   Oh, really?

AR   Yes. And actually, over the last year I started to interpret the motto as referring to the public, not to the company, like: "Don't be evil and you have nothing to fear" – like a directive to the people, but obviously it seems they have simply stopped using it. I must admit that I was also more hopeful when we started having this conversation, but at the moment I'm extremely pessimistic.

SH   I think one of the things that made us hopeful was that we felt there were some areas of technology where civil society had some semblance of control. The problem is it's becoming clearer that our control is eroding and technology is infiltrating every sphere of society, so the avenues for self-determination, even with good technical people, is reducing every day.

RA   And, of course, these new technologies have been built on top of existing social and economic inequality. The problems that we had 40 years ago we still have now: racism, unequal distribution of wealth, corrupt oligarchies... and now we are just putting a layer of technology on top of that. It's not going to fix what's underneath, and actually the global poor are becoming more disenfranchised, more disempowered, and more angry. No technological fix will be able to address that.

SH   And these global tech companies are hoovering up all the good people working in tech. One of the people from Whisper Systems, the company that produces free, open source and secure applications like Signal, has recently joined Google. There'll be nobody left soon.

RA   Also in Latin America, I have seen all the good activists, all the good social justice lawyers, all the good people, are either under-resourced or they get these great job offers with these companies, and they cannot say no. They have families and they are fed up with living a precarious life, and they know that the government cannot offer them anything. Unless we think creatively and find a place for such people, so that they won't be tempted to switch sides, we are toast.

A UTOPIAN EMPTINESS

JF   Can you give any examples of a potential counter-power to a Silicon Valley? Are there some new political parties or political movements, or new forms of organization that seem to be effective?

AR   There is some potential, especially on a local level, to connect local groups who are coping with concrete, local problems, to help them find answers to them. That is one thing. But I think what we really need is to develop new models of utopia. This world is dominated by Silicon Valley's ideology. Ok, China is coming but China is just adopting the same ideology and practices so that's not an alternative. There's a real lack of utopian thinking. For one thing, we can't bring socialism back, that's really over, you know. I think it's just not attractive to people anymore. And socialist ideology is rooted in a historical situation very different from our own. What gives me hope is that people are clearly not fulfilled and not satisfied by consumerism. People in the Western world still take more anti-depressants than anywhere else and people are not really happy.

At some point I hope that this Brave New World, when it reaches its absolute apex, will be revealed in all its emptiness. There is a spiritual emptiness to Silicon Valley's ideology because it tells people that they are superfluous and that machines will rule the world. Is this a Utopia? No! It's just a slap in the face of humanity. So, maybe at some point society will reach a point of no return, and, as in past centuries, people will come up with another way to organize life. At the moment there is a real void.

SH   Yeah, I agree, I think that we're going to have to get to a stage where things become much worse before most people will come to understand the severity of our situation. The problem is that people are too comfortable at present. So many of these developments that we find troubling, for 90% of people they're OK because they're comfortable, it's not their problem, so then why bother to change it? And, as you say, "socialism" has become just a dirty word, which is perhaps another victory of propaganda. We have no alternative and yet democracy doesn't work. Our democratic systems clearly aren't functioning but currently we have no other option.

AR   Socialism also emerged as a response to industrialization. We need, a different kind of socialism. Socialism arose in a very materialistic world, which was necessary at that point in history as a corrective to the religious worldview. But now we need something else, something that is deeply rooted in humanity.

MAKING EXCLUSION VISIBLE

RA   You said that ninety percent of people are comfortable with things – but the reality is that the majority of people are still outside this Silicon Valley system.

AR   That's true.

RA   I think that we are seeing the building of a kind of fortress, with all these hypnotized zombies in their smart homes, living inside a bubble and peripheral populations left on the outside. That's what I see. I mean, it's a little bit like in Delhi where you see these very nice neighborhoods, that are isolated and insulated. And all the poverty of the city is hidden - out of sight, out of mind. I think that it is good to dismantle the idea that the technological utopia will benefit all, that the benefits of the digital age will reach everyone. These benefits are not for all and we have to make the exclusion visible and understand how our rights are being progressively eroded. For instance, we need to start educating children about data properly. We need to help them to see that data collection is a form of expropriation, and to teach them about technology from a very early age. Not everyone has to be a coder but everyone should know the basics and be able to understand governmental and corporate collection of everybody's data.

SH   Yes, it's important to understand the data.

RA   We need to think about how we can embed rights in code, about how we can embark on creating a new legal design. Because at the moment what we have is a situation where those in power – the educators, judges, data protection authorities – none of them understand because they don't really understand new tech.

SH   You can see it when parliaments debate new surveillance laws.[63]

RA   In Germany even,

SH   In the UK, lawmakers just don't understand what they're saying regarding information technology.

RA   But people, especially the global poor, they understand what expropriation means, they understand what exploitation means, and they understand what colonization means.

SH   And that's basically what we are creating, it's a two-tiered global system of the privileged and the non-privileged.

---

63. The Guardian: "The Guardian view on the draft investigatory powers bill: snooper's charter 3.0" 2015 https://archive.is/2v1n5
UK Investigatory Powers Act 2016 https://archive.is/hBFN7
Article 19: Germany: "New Law enabling surveillance of foreign citizens threatens freedom of expression." 2016 https://archive.is/70h2O

RA   And because people in the global south understand these concepts we see a much bigger reaction there than in the West. Because if you don't understand the way your rights are being trampled you're trapped in this bubble.

SH   Yeah, and people in the West are constantly being fed pro-paganda by a media system that works with government to try to make them believe that surveillance is a good thing and necessary to protect people. And in the case of Google, nobody even needs convincing that they are great, because they seem to provide a service for free, people don't seem to understand what is being taken away from them in the process of using Google's platforms.

INACTION IS NOT AN OPTION

JH   Is there any specific topic, which you think we should cover in more concrete terms? Maybe something about hope? We have seen that things seem to be deteriorating – more terrorist attacks, the loss of civil liberties, Julian is still sitting in the embassy,[64] Edward Snowden is still in Moscow[65] – when you look to the next couple of years, how do you see the future?

64. During the high profile publication of classified documents from the US government in 2010, Julian Assange was embroiled by the Swedish police in a legal case involving allegations of sexual misconduct. Given permission to leave Sweden, he relocated to the UK whereupon the Swedish authorities issued an arrest warrant for his arrest in order to question him. He has not been charged with a crime in Sweden.

Fearing onward extradition to the United States following the announcement there of a criminal investigation into his actions as a publisher, Assange fought extradition to Sweden in the UK courts, a period during which his liberty was curtailed and he was forced to live under house arrest in the UK.

When the UK Supreme Court found against him and ordered his extradition, Assange entered the Embassy of Ecuador in London on June 19, 2012 and applied for political asylum, which was formally granted two months later.

In the years since, he remains imprisoned by the circumstances of his case: an outstanding arrest warrant from Sweden and a UK extradition order ensure he can not leave the embassy without being extradited to

RA   Every failure, I think, is a lesson. Winning elections won't necessarily constitute victory for us. I think it's more important to occupy spaces, political spaces, and get people into strategic positions where they can have access to resources and are able to attract other bright, progressive people. We don't have much time left, but I think we need a powerful task force, decentralized but bounded by solidarity, to start pushing for global and local change. We are

Sweden, risking onward extradition to the United States. Despite the repeated offers of the Ecuadorian government to facilitate questioning in the Embassy Swedish authorities refused until 2016 to progress the case, leaving Assange without a way of seeking his freedom.

In 2016, the United Nations Working Group on Arbitrary Detention issued a finding that Assange was arbitrarily detained by the refusal of the Swedish authorities to progress its case, and ordered an immediate resolution to the detention, and the payment of compensation to Assange. Although the Working Group has upheld its decision against numerous appeals by the United Kingdom and Sweden, the state parties have not arranged for Assange's detention to end.

A Swedish delegation finally traveled to London to interview Assange in 2016. At the time of publication Assange remains detained in the embassy, and the Swedish authorities have not reached a decision whether to rescind the arrest warrant and permit his freedom.

65. Following Edward Snowden's disclosures from Hong Kong about mass spying on the internet by the National Security Agency, the United States' authorities mounted an international manhunt to apprehend him and force him to face espionage charges. Snowden left Hong Kong accompanied by Sarah Harrison bound for a Latin American country, but was unable to board the next flight as they transited through Moscow when the United States cancelled his passport. Detained in the airport for weeks, with Harrison's aid Snowden applied for asylum in many countries from Russia. Eventually he was granted asylum by the Russian authorities. At the time of writing he remains in Russia.

trying with this book to communicate these concerns and make them accessible to other people in the hope that we can create, even if slowly, a critical mass that can effect real change. And even if we don't have a concrete agenda and a perfect formula for how to fix the world, inaction is not an option.

I remember when I was talking to Michael Ratner – one of our legal advisers and mentors, I was saying things like: "Oh my god, we do everything we can about the cases of Julian and Snowden and nothing changes, nothing happens". What he told me was, "You don't do that because you are going to win and you are going to solve these problems just like that. It's not easy, but you have to keep fighting because it's the right thing to do." I think that maybe that stayed with me because I'm not fighting because I'm hopeful, I'm fighting because it's the right thing to do. I'm fighting because if I have information, if I know that things are bad and I do nothing, then I am more responsible than those who do not know anything.

SH   I would agree with that. I'm politically active because I couldn't not be, rather than because I necessarily believe we're going to change much in the short term. I would agree that it's a positive thing that there are these groups like the Spanish political party, Podemos. However, I would say that there is tendency amongst such organizations to correctly point to problems without proposing any real answers. Now, I understand that coming up with answers to the problems faced by 21st century civilization is very difficult and you can't necessarily have a fully formed answer to everything but I think without answers it's very difficult to get the public interested and involved in social movements. Many people's lives are already reasonably comfortable, and for those whose lives are not, they have enough trouble just getting from day to day. There has to be a real promise of a solution for it to be worth their while getting involved in the struggle. I think that's something we should work on more within the Left; having a concept of what we would like our society to be like, even if it's not a fully developed utopia or a highly articulated model of a new political system.

AR   I agree we need something to offer to people if we want them to fight. At the moment there is this vacuum of ideas but I think that at some point it will change. That change is something that we also see in evolution - it's even a bio-logical necessity that at some point when something gets too big it will change somehow. It's just a question of time. So this is my hope, I do have some confidence in human evolution.

RA   Yes, we cannot deny that.

AR   So my hope is really like the belief in, call it evolution or the *Weltgeist* or whatever, that at some point change will happen. Maybe it won't be for five, ten, twenty or maybe a hundred years, but change will happen.

RA   Absolutely. I think if you look back in history, even igno-rant peasants lacking the most basic necessities stood up to their landlords and said, "No, we need to redefine power here." I think the current imbalance in power is so great that as a global society, we must again demand to redefine the relationships. We need a new ethics and a new set of principles. And it's already happening gradually – very slowly – but it's already happening in some places.

AR   Exactly.

RA   We shouldn't let go of what we've already gained as humanity.

AR   That's true. And I also agree with what you said before, when you said that even if you don't think we will win you should still keep fighting, because it's the right thing to do.

RA   And we shouldn't sacrifice joy. Joy is a very serious matter. We should have fun while we fight, that's something I think is really missing from our movements. I mean, if you have people in the streets chasing Pokémon, maybe we should initiate that to some extent and make our fight more fun, more engaging, and more creative. We should bring more artists in, and engage more with popular culture. We have a unique opportunity to share culture across borders and to engage in collective action across borders that we shouldn't dismiss.

SH   We need to copy the Google concepts of making what we create the best, the most fun, and the easiest to use.

RA   No, we shouldn't just imitate Google. We can do better than them because we are actually a more diverse crowd.

If that bunch of boring dudes in Silicon Valley created something so successful, a collective effort by brilliant people from all corners of the world can do something more powerful, something better.

JF   That's it. A good place to end.

ABOUT THE DISCUSSANTS

Renata Avila is a celebrated Guatemalan human rights lawyer and digital rights advocate. Specializing in Intellectual Property and Technology, her work addresses the crucial intersection between human rights, information, technological change and the power disparities between the Global North and South. As a lawyer in Guatemala, Avila has represented indigenous victims of genocide and other human rights abuses, including the prominent indigenous leader and Nobel Peace Prize Laureate Rigoberta Menchu Tum. In recent years she has played a central role in the international team of lawyers representing WikiLeaks founder Julian Assange and his staff. As part of her longstanding advocacy work in the field of Internet and Human Rights, she led with World Wide Web inventor Sir Tim Berners-Lee a global campaign to uphold human rights in the digital age in more than seventy five countries. Avila sits on the Board of Creative Commons, is a trustee of the Courage Foundation, - an organization set up to assist whistleblowers at risk - and is an advisory board member of BITS initiative for the Municipality of Barcelona, which explores the potential of decentralized technologies. She is currently based in Belgrade and Guatemala, and is writing a book on the subject of Digital Colonialism.

Sarah Harrison is a renowned British journalist and human rights defender. A former researcher with the London-based Centre for Investigative Journalism and the Bureau of Investigative Journalism, Harrison left to work at WikiLeaks during the height of its groundbreaking publication of US military and State Department documents in 2010. Pioneering and overseeing WikiLeaks' trademark collaborative media partnerships, Harrison was Investigations Editor, working at the centre of the online publisher's investigative projects for over six years. Harrison was propelled to international recognition in 2013, when, as part of WikiLeaks' rescue effort, she worked to get NSA whistleblower Edward Snowden out of Hong Kong to Moscow, where she assisted him in gaining asylum. Unable to return to England after the use of UK anti-terror laws against journalists, Harrison relocated to Berlin, where she was awarded the International Willy Brandt Prize for "special political courage" by the SPD, the German centre-left political party. Harrison is also a co-founder of the Courage Foundation, an international civil society organization set up to protect whistleblowers and truthtellers. Courage raises money for whistleblowers' legal defenses (including that of Edward Snowden) and runs their public defense campaigns.

Angela Richter is an acclaimed Croatian-German theater director, activist and author. After studying under Jürgen Flimm at the Academy of Music and Theater in Hamburg, she became a member of the Hamburg-based artist group, Akademie Isotrop. She founded the Fleet Street Theater in Hamburg in 2001, and is currently one of the four house directors at the Cologne National Theater Schauspiel Köln. She was the 2009 recipient of the Rolf-Mares Theater

Award for Best Play, with Der Fall Esra. In recent years, her work has focused on online social movements and digital activism. Her interest in WikiLeaks and Julian Assange led to the critically lauded 2012 theater piece, *Assassinate Assange,* shown in Berlin, Hamburg, Cologne and Vienna. Her groundbreaking 2014/2015 "transmedia" production, "Supernerds," was a simultaneous performance across multiple media, including internet, sudden life gaming, radio, television and live theater, exploring the topics of digital mass surveillance, whistleblowing and digital dissidents. A selection of the interviews on which the piece is based is available as *Supernerds - Conversations with Heroes* from Alexander Verlag Berlin in both German and English. Richter divides her time between Berlin and Cologne.

ACKNOWLEDGMENTS

Thanks to George Diez, Joseph Farrell, Colin Robinson and Debs.